K-12 Education

Culture and Community

K-12 Education

Culture and Community

The Van Andel Education Institute
Grand Rapids, Michigan

For all the children

Contents

Van Andel Educators Institute
An Academic Program

8

Foreword

In this volume we have attempted the difficult task of transposing thoughtful, stimulating lectures, presented in an environment where there was considerable dialogue and discussion, from the richness of the spoken word to the discipline of the printed page. These lectures were presented at the third Van Andel Educators Institute, held July 26–30, 1999, at Haworth Conference Center on the campus of Hope College in Holland, Michigan.

We had the privilege of bringing together seven lecturers from various disciplines and educators who serve as either a superintendent of a school system or a principal of a school. These superintendents and principals came from various parts of the country, from various types of schools—urban, suburban, and rural—and brought a range of personal backgrounds and experiences to the discussions.

We believe these lectures are of such quality and significance that they will be of interest to a wider audience. It is our hope that you, the reader, will confirm our judgment and that you will also sense something of the spirit of inquiry and challenge that prevailed.

These Educators Institutes are one of the programs of the Van Andel Education Institute. The Education Institute, along with a companion organization, the Van Andel Research Institute, are the operating arms of the Van Andel Institute, founded in 1996 by Jay and Betty Van Andel as the vehicle for accomplishing their major long-term philanthropic goals in education and medical science research.

Dr. Luis A. Tomatis, a distinguished cardiac surgeon who retired in 1996, serves as president and COO of both the Research and Education Institutes. Soon after assuming these responsibilities, he invited me to play a role in shaping the direction and programs of the Van Andel Education Institute. I had been retired from the presidency of Hope College for nine years, but this was a unique opportunity, for I realized that the Institute has the potential to play a definitive role in education.

As Dr. Tomatis and I began to chart a course for the activities of the Van Andel Education Institute, we were well aware that at the national level we have major concerns related to K-12 education, and decided that our initial efforts should be focused in this area. We met with a number of national education leaders to seek their counsel on the needs of K-12 education and the role the institute might play.

From these conversations we concluded that the Van Andel Education Institute would focus initially on foundational issues such as the purposes of education, the learning process, moral and ethical issues, leadership, and the scientific and cultural developments in contemporary society that impact K-12 education. It was in this context that the concept for the Van Andel Educators Institute was developed. These Institutes have been very well received. We are pleased to present the 1999 lectures in this volume. Limited copies of the 1997, 1998, and 1999 lectures are available from the Van Andel Education Institute.

As the week of the Institute proceeded, and each of the lecturers sought to bring insights into issues that are important to leaders of education, the overall theme that emerged was "Culture and Community." Contemporary culture not only impacts the perspectives and values of students (and their parents) as they come to our schools but also is the context in which we must define our educational mission and goals. While there is, to some extent, a national culture, impacted significantly by the media, the entertainment industry, and to a lesser extent by a range of institutions, including the church, there are also local cultures, impacted by the history, vitality, economy, and ethnic makeup of the community in which the schools function. A sense of community and a sense of place are important assets in achieving our academic mission—particularly in public education.

Though we have lost much of this sense of community in recent decades, schools can play a significant role in reshaping our communities and making them places of mutual concern, a place where noble purposes and the common good are encouraged and appreciated. These themes are articulated from a variety of perspectives in the lectures that are presented in this volume.

Art and aesthetics are vital dimensions of our cultural heritage, our contemporary life, and the educational missions of our schools. We were eager to have these issues addressed in one of our Educators Institutes, and this year we were privileged to have Professor Nicholas Wolterstorff, the Noah Porter Professor of Philosophical Theology at Yale University, give two lectures on the theme of "Two Ways of Thinking About Art." His historical and philosophical approach provides perceptive insights into the role of art in society and a foundation on which schools can develop creative programs to engage all students in the arts.

The most difficult context in the United States today in which educators are called to offer quality education is the urban sections of our large cities. These systems are very large, serve many students from minority groups where poverty abounds, and many of these systems have been poorly managed over the years. Two of our lecturers had major leadership roles in bringing significant renewal to such school systems.

Dr. Beverly Hall, who began her new position as Superintendent of Atlanta Public Schools a few weeks before the Institute, gave an overview of her experiences while serving as the state-appointed Superintendent of Newark Public Schools after the State of New Jersey took over the school system. Her lecture, "Lessons Learned—Newark Four Years Later," was very well received. Her courage, wisdom, and dedication in the context of the complex and difficult situation into which she was called elicited the admiration of all who heard her presentation.

Ms. Maribeth VanderWeele, who began her career as a jour-
nalist covering education in the Chicago area, now serves as
Inspector General of the Chicago Public Schools after the city of
Chicago took over the management of this very large school system.
In her lectures, "Surviving Bureaucracy" and "Dealing with the News
Media," she presented her insights into the renewal that has occurred
and reflected on her involvement and her world view, which has
guided her approach to addressing difficult issues.

At this Institute we were privileged to have lectures from two
eminent social scientists: Dr. Robert Wuthnow, the Gerhard R.
Andlinger Professor of Social Sciences and Director of the Center for
the Study of Religion at Princeton University, and Dr. David G.
Myers, the John Dirk Werkman Professor of Psychology at Hope
College. Dr. Wuthnow, a sociologist, has gained national recognition
for his studies of contemporary American society, very effectively uti-
lizing both survey and in-depth interviews. In his lecture "The
Fragmenting of America," he cites many evidences of the fragmentation in American society, articulates the cultural trends that give rise
to this fragmention, and reflects on some ethical responses that can
mitigate this trend, including the role of religion in promoting an
ethical response and encouraging personal spiritual discipline in a
scociety that provides abundant freedom.

In his second lecture, "Teaching Forgiveness," Dr. Wuthnow
noted that a fragmented society generates many situations in which
people feel betrayed. It is in this context that teaching forgiveness has
special significance. On the basis of his current research on forgiveness, Dr. Wuthnow cites a number of misunderstandings about forgiveness and his conviction that through deliberate effort, forgiveness
can become an effective dimension of our lives. He offered some
reflections on the organizations in society, including schools, that can
play a role in teaching forgiveness.

Dr. Myers' lecture, "The American Paradox," is based on his
forthcoming book of the same title. The paradox Dr. Myers cites is
that while economically most Americans are far better off than they

have ever been, almost every indicator of societal health shows a marked downward trend over the last three decades. A social psychologist, Dr. Myers has reached these conclusions based on extensive research data from many sources. His findings document the profound changes that have taken place in society in recent decades, changes that have profound implications for K-12 educators.

The final two lectures in this volume were presented by Mr. William Johnson, a landscape architect by training who is internationally recognized for his creative work in community planning. In his first lecture, "Community-Building—New Insights from an Old Art," he presented his approach to community planning—an approach that is applicable to other planning activities—which stresses creative input from many sources, speed in moving forward, and significant ownership by participants at the conclusion of the planning process. He illustrated these ideas by presenting the renewal of an inner-city neighborhood in Ann Arbor, Michigan, and development of Prairie Crossing, Illinois, a new suburb north of Chicago. In his second lecture, "Designing Memorable Place—Relating Vision to Action," he illustrated his approach to planning by reference to the renewal of the downtown in Holland, Michigan. His overall message to educators is for schools to accept their roles as important participants in building strong communities.

We are deeply grateful to these lecturers for allowing their words to be printed and made available to a larger audience, and for their invaluable help in editing them for the printed page. We extend our profound thanks and deep gratitude to them for joining us in this search for sound insights into the fundamentals of K-12 education, for their thought-provoking lectures, and for their role in the creative discussions that followed.

It is with genuine appreciation that I express my gratitude to Jane Haradine for her invaluable help in publishing this volume. She provided superb editing and many creative suggestions in bringing this effort to fruition. I also extend thanks to Denise DeJonge for her excellent work in transcribing the lectures. Ann Schoen, Lynn

Ritsema, Emma Brooks, and Phyllis VanderVelde provided invaluable help in various facets at the Institute and in preparing these lectures for publication. We are also deeply grateful for Dr. Tomatis's encouragement and sound counsel as these Institutes have developed over the past three years.

Gordon J. Van Wylen
Trustee and Director
Van Andel Education Institute

Van Andel Institute

The Van Andel Institute was founded in 1996 by Jay and Betty Van Andel as the vehicle through which they would fulfill their dream of a lasting legacy that will enrich the lives and enhance the health of generations to come. The vision for the institute is rooted in Jay and Betty Van Andel's religious faith and their concern for the well-being of their fellow humans. This is a legacy that their children—Nan, Steve, David, and Barbara—are committed to perpetuating.

As a cofounder of Amway, Jay Van Andel brought clarity of vision and great personal energy to this very successful endeavor. He served as chairman of the U.S. Chamber of Commerce and as North American chairman of the Netherlands American Bicentennial Commission.

Betty Van Andel played a major role in advancing the arts in West Michigan and in bringing Opera Grand Rapids into the limelight. She served on the board of Pine Rest Christian Hospital, one of the largest mental health centers in West Michigan.

The generosity of Jay and Betty Van Andel to a wide range of institutions and cultural endeavors in the Grand Rapids area has greatly enriched the quality of life for residents. Through the Van Andel Institute, their compassion and concern for others will have new dimensions and embrace both national and international perspectives.

The Van Andel Institute is dedicated to two major fields: medical science research and education. The medical science research is conducted through the Van Andel Research Institute (VARI). A five-member Board of Scientific Advisors, four of whom are Nobel Laureates, has been appointed to guide the activities of VARI. Dr. George J. VandeWoude, who has had a distinguished career as scientist and administrator of the National Institutes of Health, has been named Research Director of the Van Andel Research Institute. A major research facility, designed by the distinguished architect Raphael Vinoly, is under construction in Grand Rapids on the campus of Spectrum Health. The research activities will focus on molecular biology and genetics and will include clinical research.

The Van Andel Education Institute is dedicated to making definitive contributions to achieving excellence in education. One initiative involves addressing foundational issues in K-12 education, such as the purposes of education, leadership, the learning process, and moral, ethical, and character issues that bear on education. The focal point of this effort is the Van Andel Educators Institute at which leaders in education, primarily superintendents and principals, come together with distinguished educators and scholars from disciplines that bear on education for a week of study, reflection, and discussion.

The other major initiative is the Van Andel Educational Technology School (VAETS). The initial school is located at an inner-city elementary (K-6) school in Grand Rapids. A well-designed teaching facility with state-of-the-art computers and related equipment has been provided and three faculty members have been retained by VAETS. A spirit of cooperation prevails between the principal and staff of this school and the VAETS staff. The initial effort has been to enable all of the teachers and students to become computer literate. The overall goal is to use this technology to enhance the learning process throughout the curriculum. A longitudinal study is under way to measure the long-term impact of this approach. Plans are being developed to involve parents and the surrounding community in this effort.

Each of the three institutes—Van Andel Institute, Van Andel Research Institute, and Van Andel Education Institute—is governed by a board of directors. David Van Andel, a senior vice president at Amway, serves as Chairman of the Board and CEO of each of the Institutes. Luis A. Tomatis, recently retired after a distinguished career as a cardiac surgeon, serves as President and COO of the Research and Education Institutes. Mr. Van Andel and Dr. Tomatis are both deeply committed to the vision of Jay and Betty Van Andel and to ensuring that their dream of enriching the lives of future generations is fulfilled with distinction and honor.

A Message from the Chairman

As my parents moved along in years, they searched for ways to give something positive and meaningful back to the community and to society at large. The Van Andel Institute was created to enable them to do just that.

Our family has long been aware of the importance of good education, not only for personal fulfillment but also for the key role that education plays in helping us all become responsible citizens in the communities where we live and work. Over the years we have provided financial support for Christian education and for higher education at several institutions. Our present focus is on basic education—K-12 education.

While the views expressed are not necessarily those of the VAEI, we are very grateful to the lecturers and participants for the ways in which they bring focus and perceptive insights into a range of issues of vital importance to education. It is a privilege to publish the lectures presented at the 1999 Educators Institute.

We offer this book to you, hoping that by making this information available to a wider audience, the insights presented under the Institute's banner will become a positive factor in efforts to enhance and strengthen K-12 education. Improving education for all children is one of the most significant endeavors that we as a nation can undertake and in which we as individuals can be involved.

David Van Andel
Chairman
Van Andel Institute

Van Andel Educators Institute

An Academic Program

Dr. Nicholas Wolterstorff
Noah Porter Professor
of Philosophical Theology
Fellow, Berkeley College
Yale University

In his distinguished career as a scholar and teacher of philosophy, Dr. Wolterstorff has addressed a wide range of issues and published fifteen books and numerous articles in both professional and popular journals.

While serving on the faculty of Calvin College in Grand Rapids, Michigan, for thirty years, he was appointed visiting professor or guest lecturer at a number of distinguished universities. In 1989 he was appointed to his current position at Yale University.

Dr. Wolterstorff received his A.B. from Calvin and his Ph.D. from Harvard University.

Nicholas Wolterstorff

Chapter 1

Two Ways of Thinking About Art: I

In a recent book by music educator David J. Elliott, which he punningly titles *Music Matters: A New Philosophy of Music Education,* the author observes that "the basic premises of [his] book are that in order to explain the nature of music education and why it matters, we must first understand what music is and why music matters." Earlier he gave a somewhat more explicit statement of the connection he sees between the nature and significance of music education, on the one hand, and the nature and significance of music itself, on the other: "The nature of music education depends on the nature of music," and "the significance of music education depends on the significance of music in human life. If we can develop a cogent concept of what music is and why it matters, we can offer a reasonable explanation of what music education is and why it matters."

What Elliott says here seems to me indubitably true—and true not just of music but of all the arts. Before we can settle on the nature and worth of a program in poetry education, for example, we have to have views concerning the nature of poetry and its significance in human life. Differing views on the nature and significance of poetry will inevitably yield differing views as to how we should go about educating students in poetry, and differing views as to its place in the curriculum.

I dare say that when it comes to the role of the arts in school education, questions as to the nature and significance of the arts are scarcely at the forefront of the attention of school superintendents and principals. What they are most vividly aware of is public controversies concerning the arts. One group of parents suggests that the budget deficit be eliminated by scrapping all programs in music; another observes that far more money is spent on the football team than on musical groups, and that accordingly the football program should be eliminated. One group of parents protests the novels being assigned in one of the English classes, while another insists that for students not to have read Salinger and his like is for them to be uncultured. And so forth.

Of course it would be folly to downplay the significance of such controversies; they can virtually immobilize an educational system. Yet I suggest that, in the long run, the controversies to which Elliott alludes are far more important.

Be it granted that our local school will have a music program and a program for the visual arts. What's to be done in these programs? And how do these programs fit into the curriculum as a whole? Any answers to those questions presuppose some understanding of the nature and significance of the arts.

That, then, is what I want mainly to talk to you about in these two sessions: the nature and significance of the arts. In this first talk I propose discussing that way of thinking about the arts which has been prominent in the West now for some two centuries and which, so Elliott argues, lies behind the dominant recent philosophy of music education. Elliott's concern is exclusively with music education; he makes no claim beyond that. But I would generalize: that same way of thinking about the arts to which Elliott calls attention seems to me to have played an important formative role in educational programs for the arts generally.

In my second talk, I want to propose and defend an alternative way of thinking about the arts. Anyone who is a writer is naturally gratified by the sight of those who take up one's ideas and run with them. In various earlier writings of mine, I laid out the outlines of that alternative way of thinking about the arts which I will be setting before you in our second session; a few other writers have laid out similar proposals. It's this alternative way of thinking about the arts to which Elliott appeals in the proposals he makes for rethinking and reconfiguring music education.

The contemporary perspective on the arts

It's commonly taken for granted that what we find true of the arts as we know them is true of humanity's art in general. This is true not only for lay people but for professional philosophers and theorists of the arts as well. Let me give one or two examples.

Some years back, during a break in a conference on the arts that I was attending, I got to talking with the director of a New York gallery. In the course of our conversation he happened to remark that he saw less and less leisure in our society, and that made him concerned about the arts, since where there is no leisure, there is no art. I nodded agreement.

For some reason his remark stuck in the forefront of my mind, and during the subsequent session, instead of listening to the speaker, I began mulling over what this gallery director had said. Suddenly his remark changed its colors. Instead of looking like a bland truism, it appeared to me obviously false, at least if taken as a statement about humanity's art generally, which is how he had formulated it. Consider the work songs of the world. You and I don't do much singing while working; given what we do and where we do it, it would be a distraction to ourselves and a nuisance to others. But in other times and places, people did a great deal of singing while working. What's needed for work songs is not leisure, but work. Or think of those wonderfully designed quilts of the Pennsylvania Amish, of which there has recently been an exhibition in a New York gallery. It seems odd to describe the Amish women as spending their leisure time making these quilts; in their economy, if there were to be quilts, the women had to make them. I suppose it took them a bit more time to make beautiful quilts in place of dumpy ordinary ones, but this was their work. The beauty emerged not from how they spent their leisure, but from how they did their work.

Or consider the statement I heard by a speaker at another conference on the arts to the effect that since liturgical art is art in service of the church, it represents art not yet come into its own. Clearly, what the speaker had in mind, as art come into its own, was concert hall music, museum art, and reading room poetry. My initial response to this comment was to regard it, too, as a bland truism; yes, liturgical art does represent art not come into its own. But, as on that earlier occasion, something about the statement led me to stop listening to what else the speaker had to say in order to mull over that one statement. It, too, changed its colors. Instead of looking like a bland truism, it began to look very strange. Why does liturgical art represent art not come into its own? Granted, liturgical music is not concert hall music, but why conclude from this that it represents music not come into its own?

Some years back I read about a research project which demonstrated, so the researchers claimed, that cows tend to give more milk when classical music of certain kinds is played while they are being milked. Mozart seems to have been especially effective, more so, as I recall, than Beethoven. The researchers didn't try Stravinsky, but I think I can guess what Stravinsky would do to cows! Now it seems right to describe Mozart played so as to get cows to give more milk as Mozart's music not come into its own; Mozart's music was never meant for this. But why think of liturgical music along the lines of classical music played for cows? After all, liturgical music was meant for liturgy. If one puts it to some other use—the use of the concert hall, for example—it's then that it isn't doing what it was meant to do. It's then that it isn't coming into its own.

I could give other examples, but that would be "piling on." My point is this: Those of us who are members of the intelligentsia and the professional class in our society operate with a generally shared way of thinking about humanity's art. Though most of the time we simply take this way of thinking for granted, every now and then we bring it to the surface by enunciating what we regard as truisms that we expect everyone to assent to. Much of this way of thinking about the arts is not truistic at all; much of it is in fact false. It has not been arrived at by simply absorbing the nature and significance of humanity's art and then expressing what we have absorbed.

What's going on instead is this: In the eighteenth century and the early part of the nineteenth, a revolution took place among us in the West in our characteristic way of engaging with and thinking about the arts. Most of us do our thinking about the arts, and our acting within the arts, in the context of that revolution. Our way of thinking about the arts is historically situated and determined.

The contemplation model

Perhaps the most important part of the eighteenth-century revolution was the emergence into dominance of what I shall call the "contemplation model" for thinking about the arts. Writing about the arts in the West goes all the way back into Greek antiquity. Before the eighteenth century, such writing was for the most part focused on the making of art—the making being what we would call "composing" or "performing." Much of it consisted of offering advice to poets, musicians, painters, architects, and so forth as to how to practice their art—that is, their craft. Aristotle's *Poetics* is an example in point. After reflecting a bit on the nature of poetic drama, Aristotle spends most of his time offering advice to the poet concerning the construction of a drama. Beginning early in the eighteenth century, this all changed. The focus of attention in writings about the arts shifted dramatically from artist to public, from producer to consumer.

This shift of attention from the artist who makes to the public who uses was not sufficient, however, to make the contemplation model dominant, for there are other modes of engagement of the public with art than contemplation. Those in the Eastern Orthodox tradition of Christianity did not then, and do not now, typically treat their icons as objects of contemplation; instead they catch them up into their practices of piety and devotion. They kneel before them, kiss them, light candles in front of them. So, too, the altarpieces of the medieval Western church were not merely contemplated but caught up into the practices of Catholic piety. That, of course, explains why so many Protestants thought they smelled not just heresy and impropriety but idolatry.

The eighteenth-century theorists were surely aware of this devotional way of using painting and sculpture. But they paid it no attention. They don't bother to mention it. Art, they assumed and said, was for contemplation. Art belongs not to the active life, but to the contemplative life—not to the *vita activa* but to the *vita contemplativa*. It was this way of thinking about the arts that was reflected by that New York gallery director when he said that art requires leisure.

By using the Latin phrase *"vita contemplativa,"* I mean to suggest that the mode of engagement with, and of thinking about, art which came to prominence in the eighteenth century amounted not just to an episode in the history of art but also to an episode in the history of that way of life which has periodically been praised and practiced ever since Plato—viz, the contemplative life. It was a startling innovative episode. Plato had urged us to turn away from the sensory world and, by means of Reason, to contemplate the realm of abstract Forms. Augustine similarly had urged us to turn inward toward the soul, and then upward toward God.

By contrast, what the eighteenth-century theorists called for was *perceptual* contemplation. Naturally they did not understand this as empty-headed listening and staring; one has to use one's mind. But one also has to use one's body, one's senses. To contemplate works of musical and dramatic art, one has to use one's ears; to contemplate works of visual and literary art, one has to use one's eyes. Not turn inward and upward. Behind the eighteenth-century revolution was a radically different estimate of the worth of the physical and the sensory from what one finds in Plato and Augustine.

But back to the other way of looking at what happened, namely, as an episode in the history of the arts. The eighteenth-century theorists, by making the contemplative model dominant in their thinking about the arts, were elevating perceptual contemplation over all other uses of art. This becomes even more clear when we add one more ingredient to the mix. The eighteenth-century theorists did not just urge contemplation, they urged *disinterested* contemplation, as they called it. Disinterested contemplation of works of art was what they celebrated.

What's that? Good question! The attempt to explain what disinterestedness amounted to occupied them throughout the century; over and over they kept coming back to it. It can plausibly be argued that even at the end of the century, they had not succeeded in giving an adequate explanation. It's not hard to catch a glimpse, though, of what they were trying to get at. All of us are invested in the world in countless ways; we have "interests," concerns, desires. One of my interests right now is to explain briefly to you that new way of thinking about the arts which emerged in the eighteenth century. Perhaps one of yours is to get enough exercise these next few days to compensate for the overeating one inevitably does at conferences.

What the eighteenth-century theorists urged on their readers is contemplation of works of art which is not done for the sake of interests. My way of being invested in the world is not to be employed as my reason for listening to music, for looking at the painting, for reading the poetry. My contemplation is to be entirely disinterested.

But if I set all my interests off to the side, what reason remains for me to listen, look, or read? Well, if I don't engage in perceptual contemplation so as to achieve some interests of mine, there is nothing left but to do so for the sake of the contemplation itself. The worth of the contemplating has to be found in the contemplating. Not in any benefits *yielded* by the contemplating—increase in knowledge, moral improvement, emotional stability, whatever—but in the benefits of the contemplating.

And that benefit, so these theorists thought, could be nothing else than the *delight* of the contemplating. One is to listen, look, and read for the sake of the delight to be experienced in listening, looking, reading. "Why are you reading that book?" "I'm reading it because I like reading it." That's a good eighteenth-century answer.

And what if you like reading it because it's by your good friend Martha. Martha has been talking for years about the novel she was working on. You didn't believe she would ever get it finished, let alone find a publisher. But she did, so you're happy for her; and you're finding what she wrote was surprisingly different from what you expected, and much better.

No, that won't do. Interests are still rearing their ugly heads; you haven't put them off to the side. If you weren't invested in Martha the way you are, you wouldn't be experiencing the delight that you are.

The delight in the contemplating must be as disinterested as the contemplating. Or better, the fact that your delight is not truly disinterested shows that your contemplation is not truly disinterested.

The elitist dimension

But what's to be the focus of our delight then? If I'm to put out of my mind that this is my friend Martha's novel, and that at several points I find it surprising that she could or would have written a passage like this, what must I pay attention to? Well, in reading a novel you're to pay attention just to internal plot structure, character development, etc. Listening to music you're to attend just to the internal sound patterns of the music and to whatever may be the intrinsic character of those patterns. In looking at a painting you're to attend just to the internal pattern of colors and textures and to whatever intrinsic character those may have. Eventually the eighteenth-century theorists called such qualities *aesthetic* qualities; they called disinterested contemplation "aesthetic contemplation," and the delight one experiences in aesthetic contemplation they called "aesthetic delight." Our concept of the aesthetic was born in the eighteenth century.

But what's the point? Who cares? The fact that the eighteenth-century theorists spent so much time and energy trying to distinguish aesthetic contemplation from other ways of engaging the arts indicates that either they regarded it as a terribly bad way of engaging the arts or as an exceptionally good way. Otherwise, what difference does it make whether one's way of listening to music is aesthetic or not? Why spend so much time picking out the aesthetic way of engaging the arts except either to warn people away from it or to urge them toward it?

We know, of course, that the reason the eighteenth-century theorists spent so much time and effort trying to explain what they meant by the aesthetic way of engaging in the arts—the way of disinterested contemplation—is that they thought this way important. They wanted to celebrate it, to urge it on their readers. What I want to indicate now is that their reason for doing so was unmistakably elitist.

One of the best ways to see this is to look at a passage from a piece that Joseph Addison published on June 21, 1712, in his daily London newspaper, *The Spectator*. The passage is charmingly written, and I want to read it to you. But its English is by now old-fashioned—it was, after all, written almost three hundred years ago—and it's easy to miss the significance of what Addison is saying. So let me provide a bit of context and preliminary explanation.

In the piece from which the passage is taken, Addison speaks several times of "polite persons." In your and my English, a polite person is a person of good manners. But that's not what Addison means. What he means by a polite person is what you and I would call a "cultured" person, a person of culture, or, to use the German expression, a person of *Bildung*.

A new social ideal was emerging in Addison's day, the ideal of the cultured person. Think of it like this. We all operate with the concept of social roles: the role of the clergy, the role of the professional athlete, the role of the public intellectual, the role of the high school teacher, the role of the superintendent of schools, and so forth. Each of us regards certain of these roles as more admirable than others, and often there will be considerable agreement within a society concerning the worth of certain roles. Ancient Athenian society, for example, greatly admired the role of public orator. Contemporary American society greatly admires the role of entrepreneurial businessman and professional athlete, while having virtually no admiration for the role of politician and little for that of school teacher.

The significance of Addison's comments is that he is addressing himself to those in his society who admire the newly formed role of cultured person, and arguing that to be a cultured person, one must be a person of taste, that is, a recognizer and lover of aesthetic excellence. Now and then in earlier societies one finds considerable admiration for the role of maker of art; in the city-states of Renaissance Italy, for example, there was considerable admiration for painters. But speaking now only of the West, I'm not aware that before the eighteenth century, in England, Holland, and France, the role of cultured person of fine taste was ever a significant social ideal. Throughout Europe there had for many centuries been the role of aristocrat, and no doubt for many in society this functioned as a social ideal. But the role of cultured person was different. Many members of the aristocracy were anything but cultured persons, and, conversely, one could become a cultured person without being a member of the aristocracy. It was a social ideal appropriate to the newly emerging bourgeois democratic society. A businessman of humble origins could be a cultured person. It all depended on what he did after hours.

Now if being a cultured person is an admirable thing to be, as Addison clearly assumes it is, and if being a cultured person requires recognizing aesthetic excellence and enjoying it, then presumably there's something admirable about aesthetic delight—something admirable about the delight one experiences when engaged in disinterested contemplation of beautiful objects. What might that be? Addison's answer is both fascinating in its content and charming in its expression. I'll put into my own words what Addison is saying, but first let me allow him to speak to you in his own voice. Not everything will be immediately intelligible since, as I mentioned before, the English is by now old-fashioned, but the charm of Addison's rhetoric will be unmistakable. His main topic is what he calls "the pleasures of the imagination," that is, the pleasures of experiencing beauty. Recall that he is addressing himself to "polite" people, or to people who would like to become "polite" if they are not already that. This is what he says:

> The pleasures of the imagination ... are not so gross as
> those of Sense, nor so refined as those of understanding.
> The last are, indeed, more preferable, because they are
> founded on some new knowledge or improvement in the
> mind of Man; yet it must be confessed, that those of the
> imagination are as great and as transporting as the other ...
> a description in Homer has charmed more readers than a
> chapter in Aristotle. Besides, the pleasures of the imagina-
> tion have this advantage, above those of the understanding,

that they are more obvious, and more easier acquired.... A man of a polite imagination is let into a great many pleasures, that the vulgar are not capable of receiving.... There are, indeed, but very few who know how to be idle and innocent.... A man should endeavour, therefore, to make the sphere of his innocent pleasures as wide as possible, that he may retire into them with safety, and find in them such a satisfaction as a wise man would not blush to take. Of this nature are those of the imagination, which do not require such a bent of thought as is necessary to our more serious employments, nor, at the same time, suffer the mind to sink into that negligence and remissness, which are apt to accompany our more sensual delights, but like a gentle exercise to the faculties, awaken them from sloth and idleness, without putting them upon any labour of difficulty. We might here add, that the pleasures of the fancy are more conducive to health, than those of the understanding, which are worked out by dint of thinking, and attended with too violent a labour of the brain.

Addison sets the whole realm of ordinary activity—of "business," as he calls it—off to the side without comment. For him, being a person of culture pertains not to what one does when engaged in one's own business, but to what one does after hours—to what one does with one's leisure, one's "idleness," as he calls it. Addison considers three options. One may spend one's idle hours concentrating on sensory pleasures, on intellectual pleasures, or on the pleasures of the imagination.

Addison treats sensory pleasures with disdain. They are gross, unrefined, and morally dubious; they make a wise man blush. Those who pursue them will likely sink into negligence and remissness. In short, they are the pleasures of the vulgar, that is, of the ordinary people, not of the wise and polite. Enough said.

It has to be conceded that intellectual pleasures are the noblest of all, contributing, as they do, to improvement in the mind of man. Nonetheless, there are good reasons not to recommend the pursuit of such pleasures for after-hours leisure. For one thing, it is often mind-crackingly difficult and exhausting to experience such pleasures. Perhaps reading Immanuel Kant with comprehension gives great and noble pleasure, but it is also exhausting. Intellectual pleasures, to use Addison's words, are often "worked out by dint of thinking, and attended with too violent a labour of the brain." They're dangerous to one's health. In addition, they are accessible to fewer people than are the pleasures of the imagination; not many people have what it takes to read Kant with pleasure. "A description in Homer," says Addison, "has charmed more readers than a chapter in Aristotle." The pleasures of the imagination win the day.

What shall we carry away from this excursion into Addison? Not, I would say, his quirky observations about after-hours pleasure. Rather this: from the time it first emerged in the early eighteenth century, and ever since, the contemplative model for engaging with and thinking about the arts has been associated with cultural elitism. Engaging in disinterested contemplation of the arts is what you have to do if you want to be a cultured person. Simply engaging the arts is not enough; everybody does that. Your engagement must be aesthetic. If you kiss icons but never go to museums, if you sing hymns but never go to concert halls, if you watch movies but never go to plays, if you share stories with your buddies at work but never read novels, you are not a cultured person. That may be no skin off your nose; you may be much more envious and admiring of professional athletes like Michael Jordan and of entrepreneurs like Bill Gates than of any cultured person you know. But for some people in our society, being a cultured person means a lot. And the fact that you, though engaged with the arts, are unconcerned with the aesthetic dimension is a sure sign that you are not a person of culture. The art you traffic in is not high art.

The relationship between craft and art

Let me mention one other development in our way of engaging with and thinking about the arts which took place in the eighteenth century. About this one I can be brief. When traveling in distant societies and reading about earlier ones, it's natural for us to take for granted that they are or were like us in working with a concept of the arts. After all, in every society for which we have information there was music, there was fiction, there was poetry, there was visual representation and design, there was sculpture. But not so. Our concept of *the arts* was also an eighteenth-century invention. You and I still sometimes use the word *art* as a synonym for *craft*. The *art* of furniture design and furniture-making is the *craft* of furniture design and furniture-making. Before the eighteenth century, an art was a craft. The art of music was the craft of music—specifically, the art of music-making. The art of painting was the craft of painting. And nobody saw any particular connection among what we would now call the major fine arts: music, painting, sculpture, poetry, drama. It comes as a surprise to learn that the medieval theorists regarded music as more closely related to mathematics than to painting and poetry; if they had been setting up curricular options, they would have regarded music or mathematics as a much more sensible option than music or painting. It's easy to see why they did not have our concept of the arts. The craft of making music is very different from the craft of making paintings, as are those from the craft of making poems. It's not at all likely that someone good at one of these will be good at another. If one focuses on the craft of making, our unified concept of the arts is most unlikely to emerge.

But now suppose that in thinking about music, painting, sculpture, poetry, and drama we shift emphasis from making to using; and suppose further that we focus not on uses in general but on that very special use which is disinterested perceptual contemplation; then gradually the realization will emerge that there is a very good reason to group together these five crafts, plus a few others. Within all of them we find works rewarding of aesthetic contemplation. And not only that: many of us discover that we are capable of experiencing aesthetic delight in contemplating the works of more than one of these crafts. Quite a few of us, indeed, discover that we are capable of enjoying aesthetic engagement with all of them: music, painting, sculpture, poetry, and drama. Whereas hardly anybody is good at making works in more than one of these genres, many of us are good at enjoyingly engaging in disinterested contemplation of works in all of them. Hence there emerged our concept of the arts, that is, of the fine arts. It's no longer the concept of a craft; it is instead a type of object rewarding of aesthetic contemplation.

Some final thoughts

I have told you nothing about what the eighteenth-century theorists had to say about those many ways of engaging with art other than disinterested contemplation. That's because the eighteenth-century theorists had nothing to say about these other ways except just this: those other ways of engaging with art represent art not come into its own. Art comes into its own when it is used as an object of aesthetic contemplation. Only then, so it was said, is it not subjected to one or another extraneous use; only then is it liberated, autonomous, free to follow its own inherent dynamics rather than being in the service of bishops, kings, and shopkeepers. The eighteenth-century theorists were simply not seriously interested in any art except that in which art's destiny was supposedly fulfilled. We know that Addison went to church; there he would have encountered liturgical music. One would never know it from his writings.

A good deal more could be said about that way of engaging with and thinking about the arts which we have inherited from the eighteenth-century revolution. It would be interesting, for example, to discuss the institutional base for this new way of engaging with the arts which then began to develop and is now familiar to all of us—artists putting their work on the market instead of serving patrons; and public concert halls, museums, and libraries being constructed for use by all who were (or wished to be) cultured.

It would also be fascinating to discuss an important development that took place at the hands of the nineteenth-century Romantics. They began to think of contemplative art of the cultural elite as socially other, even as salvific. Specifically, they argued that the natural sciences of the modern world, the democratic politics of the modern world, the capitalist economies of the modern world, and the rationalist religions of the modern world are all alike in that they are destructive of ancient unities. Art alone is the exception; not only does art not destroy ancient unities, it provides us with examples of unity. The Romantics speculated that for that reason it might just possibly save us—help us to knit together once again the tattered fragments of our existence in the modern world. It could only do this, however, if it remained free from the clutches of those who tried to control it and never ceased to speak prophetically to the oppressive tendencies of the modern world. I dare say all this sounds more or less familiar to you: Jesse Helms vs. the National Endowment for the Arts, 150 years ago.

But rather than further trying your already strained patience, let me bring this session to a close by returning to where I began, namely, Elliott's discussion of music education. On pages 27–28 of his book *Music Matters,* Elliott quotes several brief indicative passages from the major theorists in music education for the past forty years.

Let me in turn quote from three of them. In 1958, Harry Broudy wrote, "We are interested in music as a type of aesthetic experience. In aesthetic experience we perceive objects in order to grasp the sensuous characteristics and not *primarily* to further knowledge or useful enterprises."

In 1982 Peters and Limmer wrote, "The best use of music in schools and the best reasons for the inclusion of music in the curriculum stem from music as part of what has been known as "aesthetic education.""

And in 1989, Bennett Reimer wrote that music education "must be so arranged that aesthetic experience is central."

There is no mistaking where these writers are coming from. In saying that music education should be conducted as a component of aesthetic education, they are not giving expression to some obvious eternal truth about the arts; they are reflecting our eighteenth-century inheritance. Of course this is not to show that they are mistaken; perhaps the eighteenth-century theorists were on the right track. Perhaps the disinterested aesthetic contemplation of works of art is so far superior to all other uses as to make it the only use worth taking note of in the schools—so far superior, indeed, as to make it not worth one's time even talking about the others.

"Perhaps," I say; "I don't myself believe it for a minute." But that's for our next session.

Nicholas Wolterstorff

Chapter 2

Two Ways of Thinking About Art: II

What we were doing in the first of our two sessions, and will continue doing in this second, was engaging in a bit of philosophy of art: what is the nature of the arts, and what is their significance in human life?

An obvious question is: why would I invite you to reflect on those questions? You are assembled here as a group of school superintendents and principals. What's the point of inviting you to think philosophically about art? Of course you can't help doing some thinking about art—given that every good school and school system does something or other with the arts. But what's the point of inviting you to think philosophically about the arts?

In response I could say some such thing as that you, like all human beings, are questioning creatures, and that all questions lead ultimately to philosophical questions. Since art is part of everybody's experience, and you and I can't help asking questions about it, we'll eventually wind up with philosophical questions, so why not skip the journey and jump to the end? I could say that; but I won't.

The reason I gave at the beginning of my first talk was much more concrete and pragmatic than that, much less airy and speculative. I quoted from the recent book *Music Matters,* by prominent music educator David J. Elliott, to the effect that one cannot determine the nature of music education and its place in the curriculum without first considering the nature of music itself and its significance in human life. That, I said, seems to be true—and true not just

of music but of the arts generally. To answer questions about program and curriculum, one has to start with philosophical questions.

One way to advance from that point would have been to survey
programs in education in the arts so as to determine the dominant
views concerning the nature of arts education and its place in the curriculum; and then, in turn, to scrutinize those views so as to discern
the assumptions they make concerning the nature and human significance of the arts themselves. To have gone at it like that, how
ever, would have taken much more time than we have available to us
here, and would require expertise by me in areas where I have none—
besides which, let's be frank, it would almost certainly be boring. So
my procedure was different. I took Elliott's word for it that music
education should be conceived and structured as a branch of
aesthetic education; and I spent my time sketching out for you the
view of music, and of the arts generally, which such a view presup-
poses.

The aesthetic view of the arts

I suggested that the view presupposed is not the plain and simple truth of the matter but is a view born in the eighteenth century
and prominent among the intelligentsia of Western society ever
since. For the sake of convenience, let's call it the "aesthetic view of
the arts." The eighteenth-century theorists were convinced that in
their own place and time, art was finally coming into its own. What
they had in mind was that art, to a significant extent, was finally serving as an object of aesthetic contemplation. To be thus used was the
historical destiny of art. Art had always served a multiplicity of purposes; it continued to do so in England, Holland, and France of the
eighteenth century; it continues to do so today. But only when art
serves as an object of aesthetic contemplation does it come into its
own; only then do we attend to it for the sake of delighting in its own
interior relationships and intrinsic qualities rather than putting it in
the service of interests outside itself.

Suppose, for the sake of the argument, that we grant all this.
The question remains: Why bother? What's the big deal about

aesthetic contemplation of works of art? When somebody talks about art not yet come into its own and about art coming into its own, the natural response is to cry out: Allow it to come into its own! Who wants to keep it in servitude, bondage, and tutelage? But I submit that to respond thus is to succumb to the power of the rhetoric rather than the force of the argument. For a moment let's resist being swept along by the grand historical narrative about art coming into its own, and pose this simple but central question: What's so important about using works of art as objects of aesthetic contemplation—when humanity always has and still does engage the arts in so many other ways?

The answer the eighteenth-century theorists gave to this question was unmistakably elitist: The reason to engage in aesthetic contemplation of works of art is that such engagement is an indispensable component of being a cultured person. Different theorists fleshed this answer out in different ways. Some said that the pleasure derived from aesthetic contemplation of worthy objects is a more desirable sort of pleasure than any other; that was Joseph Addison's answer. Yet others appropriated religious language and said that aesthetic contemplation unites the tattered fragments of our existence and puts us in touch with higher realities. And this is still only a sampling. Whatever the specifics, elitism was then, and remains to this day, inextricably tied up with the aesthetic view of the arts. Somebody who does not engage in the aesthetic contemplation of works of art—or does, but does not find it rewarding—is lacking in culture. Lacking, that is, in high culture—elite culture.

An alternative view: two personal experiences

My project today is to present to you an alternative way of thinking about the arts and to do what I can to make that alternative seem plausible and attractive.

What's the best way in? Let me try the following. Some of you are of an age to share with me the following memory: standing in a row, arms linked crosswise so that one's right hand grasps the right hand of the person to one's left rather than the left hand of the person to one's right, the entire row swaying gently from side to side, eyes closed or uplifted, singing slowly "We Shall Overcome." Garbage collector and college professor, black and white, male and female, devotee of the Beatles and devotee of Beethoven, professional singer and he who can't carry a tune—all singing in unison, differences making no difference. We were united in the music because we were united in the cause of civil rights, and united in the cause because we were united in the music. We sang it on the streets, in meeting halls, around camps, in front of city halls, wherever we happened to be. We didn't go to special places to sing it. It didn't matter if there was noise in the surroundings.

Did the music give pleasure upon contemplation? Did it give delight upon disinterested listening? Dumb question. We didn't listen to it; we sang it. What it did was bring tears to the eyes and fortitude to the soul. That's what it did.

Where did the music come from? I had no idea then—and still have none. For me, at the time, it was just there. When I listen to music from the classical tradition, and music that has been absorbed into the classical tradition, I want to know who wrote it and when. Such music functions for me, as it probably does for you, as relics of musical geniuses—relics, if you will, of saints in the Order of Music. I want to know of which genius the work I'm listening to is a relic. Not so for "We Shall Overcome." Purely as a matter of curiosity I would like to know where the music came from, but over the years I have made no attempt to find out.

The words? Oh, yes, the words! They went like this:

> We shall overcome,
> we shall overcome,
> we shall overcome
> some day, some day.
> Oh, I do believe,
> we shall overcome,
> we shall overcome
> some day.

Scarcely to be numbered among the masterpieces of the English poetic tradition. What the words did is enable us all together to give voice to our determined confidence; in that lay their significance. But can you imagine standing there just reciting those bland, prosaic, repetitious words? That wouldn't do it. The music transformed those humdrum words into a moving and memorable whole.

Is it good music? That's an ambiguous question. If you mean aesthetically good, I'd say, not bad. It begins with a phrase, once repeated, which rises just a bit and then falls with a skip; then there's a phrase that rises higher before falling, with no skips either in its rising or falling; finally there's the climactic phrase which moves upward with a skip to the highest pitch in the whole composition, then falls a bit, then rises a bit again, falls a bit more, falling reluctantly, as it were, until we arrive at the lowest pitch in the entire composition. Not bad, aesthetically speaking.

But with the question whether it's good you might also mean whether the music was functionally good, that is, was it doing a good job of what it was being used to do? To that question, I would say that it was magnificent. The music takes those prosaic words and catches them up into a greater whole. The determined, hopeful, confident quality of the music itself makes the whole composition—words plus music—something immeasurably greater than the words would be by themselves. The music-plus-words enabled the group to express its determined confidence with an intensity impossible with the words by themselves. At the same time, singing it intensified that confidence. By enabling us to express our confidence, it gave us confidence. So is the music good? Yes, good for that! It wasn't accidental that it proved so popular.

Now for another memory. Though it must be about twenty years ago now, I remember as if it were yesterday the first time I heard a performance of Olivier Messiaen's *Quartet for the End of Time,* composed for the somewhat odd combination of clarinet, piano, violin, and cello. Perhaps a few of you have never heard of Messiaen; most likely some of you have never heard a performance of his *Quartet.* Not to worry. For my purposes here, that doesn't matter.

As I recall, I had heard of Messiaen, but I had no idea that he was on the way to becoming one of the giants in classical music of the second half of the twentieth century. About the piece itself, the program mentioned little more than that it was written during the Second World War when the composer was incarcerated in a German prison camp, and that the instrumentation was determined by the instruments and performers available in the camp. The program did not inform me that the composition was inspired and shaped by the book of Revelation in the New Testament; nor did I learn until quite some time later that individual movements had such titles as "Liturgy of Crystal," "In Praise of the Eternity of Jesus," and "Furious Dance of the Seven Trumpets." In short, I knew nothing at all of the mystical program attached. And though I remember thinking that little phrases sounded rather like songs of birds, though not of birds I knew, I think I must have dismissed that as accidental. I now know that it was not at all accidental; Messiaen's compositions are full of the instrumental equivalents of bird songs. What I remember is being gripped and transfixed as I sat listening. At the conclusion of the second movement, the pianist, violinist, and cellist all departed from the stage, leaving only the clarinetist to perform the third movement. That movement brought me to tears; the tears remained throughout the remainder of the performance.

Two very different pieces of music; both tear-wrenching. In the one case, I participated in the singing; in the other, I was absorbed in something like disinterested contemplation.

A broader view

The aesthetic view of the arts tells us that my mode of engagement with Messiaen's *Quartet* was much nobler than my mode of engagement with "We Shall Overcome"—that there is in fact no higher mode of engagement with the arts than the intent contemplative listening that I was practicing on the Messiaen piece. I find this claim impossible to accept. I trust I've made clear how moving I found that performance of the Messiaen *Quartet;* and you realize that

I am citing it as only one example of many similar moving experiences. I would feel deeply impoverished if I could never engage in contemplative listening to music. But many of the occasions in which I joined in singing "We Shall Overcome" were also moving experiences, and you realize that I could also cite many other moving examples of this sort. So what could possibly lead somebody to say that my mode of engaging the Messiaen composition was a nobler way of engaging music than my way of engaging "We Shall Overcome"? Is the idea that aesthetic delight is nobler than struggling for justice and singing praise to God? I refuse to accept that.

It might be said that I'm not being fair to the aesthetic view. The idea is not that contemplative listening to some piece of music is a nobler way of engaging in music than singing hymns—nor that music which serves the former use well is better than music that serves the latter use well. Perhaps it's true that all in all it's more important to struggle for justice than to experience aesthetic delight; and maybe, since "We Shall Overcome" functions better in that struggle than Messiaen's *Quartet,* we should grant that it has a more important role in human life than Messiaen's composition.

But—so it may be said—that's all beside the point. The point is that only when music serves as the object of aesthetic contemplation has it come into its own. Maybe some of the uses to which it is put when it has not come into its own are more important in human affairs. But that doesn't change the fact that only when it functions aesthetically has it come into its own.

I don't accept this argument either. For one thing, if this is all the aesthetic view comes to, it does nothing to ground the accompanying elitism. But apart from that, I think it's just confused about this business of "coming into its own." Presumably something comes into its own when it's used for the purpose it was meant for and in the way it was meant to be used. Suppose that your junior high child is using the new computer you just bought him to flatten out the leaves he has collected for his biology course. Using the computer as a dead weight isn't allowing it to come into its own; that's not what computers are for. Indeed, my children think that even my way of using my computer—namely, as a fancy typewriter—is not allowing it to come into its own. "Dad," they say, "there are all those other things it can do."

So consider a piece of music which is a hymn and the way of using it which consists of a congregation all together singing the hymn so as to praise God. Surely when the hymn is used in that way, it has come into its own; that's what it was meant for. When, on the contrary, a professional group performs it, records its performance on a CD, and I listen to it sitting by myself in my living room, then it isn't coming into its own. It wasn't meant for this—even though I might in fact find the experience of listening to it in solitude very enjoyable. By contrast, when I and a number of other people were all together sitting quietly in that concert hall and listening attentively to Messiaen's *Quartet,* then that piece of music was coming into its own; it was meant for this use. Should it be recorded and played, say, as background music in my dentist's office, then in that use it would not be coming into its own.

My point is this: it is either mental confusion or rhetorical bluff to say that the arts do not come into their own until they are used as objects of aesthetic contemplation. Works of music, of painting, of sculpture, of poetry, of fiction have always been produced, and continue to be produced, for an enormous variety of different functions. They come into their own when they are used for the function for which they were meant to be used. And to go back to my earlier point, I see no reason whatsoever to say that the aesthetic function is the best and noblest. If it's true that to be counted as cultured one must spend a considerable amount of time engaging the arts aesthetically, then my response is that there's more that's important in life than being cultured—and that some of those other important things are more important.

If the dominant way of thinking about the arts which we have inherited is unsatisfactory for the reasons indicated, and other reasons besides, what shall we put in its place? Let me present you with a sketch of an alternative.

The social practices of the arts

A feature of the aesthetic view of the arts which I have not emphasized is that it focuses on works of art—works of music, paintings, poems, and so forth. I propose, in the first place, that we reorient ourselves and, rather than giving pride of place in our thinking to the objects of art, give that instead to the activities of art. For works of art are not found objects that turn up here and there on the beach. They are, from their very inception, embedded in human activity. They are the products of human activity, it takes human activity to perform or present them, and our modes of engagement with them are modes of human activity.

Let me add an important qualifier. The word "activity" has connotations which are wrong here. Of course there's something right about the word, or I wouldn't have used it—not even as a stage on the road to something better. But to my ear it suggests that the activities of art are discrete—atomistic—and most certainly they are not that. My preferred word is "practices." Rather than giving pride of place in our thinking about the arts to objects of art, I propose that we give pride of place to the practices of art—more specifically, the social practices.

What do I have in mind by practices? Let me give some examples and then make a few explanatory comments. Playing the classical guitar is a social practice; competitive ice figure-skating is a social practice; playing shortstop in baseball is a social practice; furniture-making is a social practice. Practices involve skills, but they are always more than skills. They are "arts"—in the old sense of that word. There's the art of playing classical guitar, the art of figure-skating, the art of playing shortstop, the art of making furniture. By contrast, though there is such a thing as the skill of riding a bicycle, there's no such thing as the art of riding a bicycle. There may be such a thing as the art of competitive bicycle racing; I don't know.

So what is a practice—that is, an art? A practice is a socially embodied way of doing something, such that there are not only correct and incorrect, and effective and ineffective ways of doing it, but better and worse ways. Social practices provide us with ways of achieving excellence which, apart from those practices, simply don't exist. Take the social practice of playing classical guitar. There are, of course, ways of playing the guitar which are just all wrong; but once that threshold is met, we enter the region of better and worse ways of playing. We enter the region of a unique way of achieving human excellence.

These better and worse ways of performing some practice are not embedded in the nature of things. Typical of social practices is that the criteria for better and worse performances, and the modes of human excellence that those criteria make possible, change over time, that there are controversies concerning these criteria, and that there's not some right or wrong on the matter. One person thinks that one style of performance on the classical guitar is better. Another thinks another is better. Controversies erupt. Schools and traditions get formed.

Changes in criteria for excellence, and controversies concerning the criteria, have many different sources. Probably the main source, the goals people set for themselves when engaging in the practice, alter over time. New goals emerge; old goals die out. This is especially true of the fine arts. The emergence of abstract visual art in our century represented the emergence of a strikingly new, and highly controversial, goal within the ancient social practice of painting. In the arts the goals sometimes change so dramatically that for a time people refuse to recognize the new goals as even belonging to the same old art. You all have heard the exclamation: "If this is art, then my two-year-old kid is an artist!"

The impact of traditions

Hoping that I've said enough to give you a fairly good idea of what I mean by social practice, let me now go on to make an observation about practices which, for our purposes here, will be of first importance. Practices have histories. More specifically, they have traditions. They are handed down from one person to another, from one generation to another. Thus people learn practices. They aren't born into them; they are inducted into them. Typically a person learns some practice by a combination of modeling and explicit teaching.

To learn a practice is, of course, to pick up the skills which go into that practice; but since practices are more than skills, what's learned is always more than just skills. What's learned are goals for the practice and the standards for excellence which accompany those goals. Of course the student may eventually go beyond her models and teachers in this regard. She may even rebel against them. She may aim at different goals and adopt different criteria of excellence. But she knows that's what she's doing—going beyond or rebelling against. If she has no idea whatsoever as to the goals of previous practitioners, and none regarding their criteria of excellence, then she has not yet been inducted into the practice. She has not yet learned it.

Three interlocking practices of the arts

All of this has been completely general. It's time to show how this concept of social practices applies to the arts. I have already suggested that instead of thinking of the arts as consisting primarily of works, we think of the basic reality of the arts as consisting of social practices. As a refinement of this general idea, I now propose that we think of each of the arts as consisting of three interlocking practices: composing, performance or display, and engagement or use.

I've been using music as my principal example, so let me continue. People don't in general just up and start composing music. The romantic image of the composer is that of someone who, in late adolescence, holes himself up in a tiny room somewhere and expresses himself by pouring out onto paper the sounds that he somehow finds swirling around in his mind. The reality is almost always very different. But even if that's how it does go in rare cases, that adolescent genius in the attic today is using models; the compositions he produces sound for all the world like recent Western music, not like

ancient Persian music. Composers are inducted into a compositional tradition. They learn composing—some just by using
models, most by having teachers of composition. A good part of
what they learn are goals for the process and criteria for judging better and worse products of the compositional process—better and
worse compositions.

Performance is likewise a social practice. Again, nobody is born
knowing how to perform music. We learn how to do it: learn by
modeling, learn by being taught. And once again, though skills are
obviously a large part of what goes into being a performer, what has
to be learned in learning to be a performer are the appropriate goals
and criteria for judging how well one has done. Now and then goals
and criteria for excellence in musical performance become topics of
great controversy—witness the controversies of the past two or three
decades over how to perform classical music of the pre-Romantic era.

Listening is also a practice. We're no more born knowing how
to listen to music than we are born knowing how to compose or perform music. We learn what to listen for, what to bring into the fore-
ground of attention and what to allow to recede into the background, what to acquire by way of contextual knowledge, etc. Partly
we learn by being taught; partly we learn on our own by repeated listening. And controversies erupt here, too. Different teachers often
teach students different ways of listening. Those teachers then debate
and argue with each other.

It may be helpful to make a few comments explicitly relating
this triple social-practice way of thinking of the arts to the aesthetic
view of the arts which I explained earlier. The social practices of the
arts—of music, of poetry, of fiction, of painting, of sculpture—go
back into the mists of antiquity, always changing, sometimes slowly,
sometimes rapidly, sometimes deliberately, sometimes not. These
social practices are often the subject of controversy over goals and
standards of excellence, sometimes enjoying consensus. But when
seen in their totality over space and time, these social practices display for us truly astounding diversity. Who could have anticipated
that so many different things could be done by ordering sounds, and

that so many different ways of achieving excellence would emerge, that so many different things could be done by applying pigments to relatively flat surfaces, and that so many modes of human excellence would emerge.

The way to think of the eighteenth-century revolution, then, is to see it as one more alteration in these ancient traditional practices, accompanied by the emergence of a line of thought meant to legitimate and justify these alterations. This is a much less dramatic and apocalyptic picture than that of the eighteenth-century theorists who, as we saw, tried to get us to believe that throughout human history the arts were straining and struggling to escape from the cocoon of their confinement, finally succeeding in the 1700s.

Perhaps the change which occurred in the eighteenth century was unusually revolutionary and dramatic. Nonetheless, given that the practices of art are always changing, the eighteenth-century changes were more of the same. In particular, those changes did not represent art come into its own. The changes which took place in the practices of art did not then, and do not now, all lead up to some grand historical climax.

A second thing to emphasize, by way of contrast to the aesthetic view of the arts, is this: I have spoken of each of the arts as representing three interlocking social practices—composition practices, performance or display practices, and engagement or use practices. In fact, when we take any one of the arts and look at one of its three interlocking practices, we find that we aren't dealing with just one practice for engaging or using, say, music, but at a multiplicity of practices. A point I made earlier bears repeating: We the public do many different things with music. We listen to it aesthetically, but we also use it to accompany work, for playing hopscotch, as background sound in shopping malls, for addressing praise to God, for dancing, for nightclub music. The use practices for music are multiple, as are the performing practices and the compositional practices. Working with a social practice view of the arts enables us to recognize this diversity without being forced to place these various practices into some sort of invidious hierarchy. I concede that some ways of using music are more important than others. Nonetheless, let's celebrate the diversity.

Educational issues

Let me close by returning briefly to educational questions. Suppose one adopts this triple social-practice way of thinking of the arts. What then would educational programs in the arts look like? How will they differ from those that aim at the cultivation of aesthetic sensitivity? And what place in the curriculum will such programs occupy? How will that differ from the place assigned by those who hold the aesthetic view of the arts?

I do not know the answers to these questions. Whereas I have spent a great deal of my time as a philosopher thinking and writing about the philosophy of the arts, I have spent very little time thinking about philosophy of education in general, or about philosophy of art education in particular. David Elliott, in the book I have now mentioned several times, *Music Matters,* has some interesting things to say on the issue of a philosophy of music education appropriate to a social practice view of the arts. I would recommend it to all of you. As for myself, rather than offering answers in these closing remarks, I will instead make some suggestions about the sort of considerations which ought to be brought into play.

I have made a big point of the fact that we are not born into the practices of art but inducted into them. We have to learn them. The basic question then is what the school can and should do by way of promoting such learning. Most such learning takes place outside the school, informally. It couldn't be otherwise. The school will want to intervene only when it judges at some point that informal learning is falling short at inducting young people into some important segment of the practices of art.

The aesthetic approach has a very clear and neat view as to where this shortfall takes place, which the school should intervene to repair. The social practices of aesthetically contemplating works of great aesthetic excellence is the most important of all the practices.

This is where art supposedly comes into its own. Society is very poor at informally inducting young people into that social practice. Though some parents do a fairly good job at informally inducting their own children into the practice, they are the exception. Accordingly, the school should focus on teaching students how to watch plays, how to listen to symphonies, how to look at paintings, how to read poems. An important corollary is that those who hold the aesthetic view want the school to do very little by way of instruction in performance. Two writers whom Elliott quotes, Leonhard and House, claim that faulty music programs include those "with undue emphasis on performance." Performing, in their view, is a matter of "skill" and "technique" rather than musical knowledge. Reimer agrees. Singing and playing instruments is merely a means to the end of making available works of music for aesthetic contemplation; one should beware of giving it a very large role in music education programs.

The social practice view—at least as I would apply it—will not dispute that teaching the practice of aesthetic contemplation of works of high art is an important part of the school curriculum. It agrees that society is not very good at informally inducting its young people into this practice, and it agrees that the practice is important. What it does not concede, however, is that this practice is always and for everybody the most important of all the use practices. Nor does it concede that works which reward this practice are always and for everybody the most important in which to engage. It insists, for example, that the liturgical use of music—singing hymns to praise God—is no less important. Nor does the social practice view concede that the importance of performance is just that it is a skill whereby works are made available for the really important thing—namely, aesthetic contemplation. It denies that performance practices are merely skills; they are, among other things, modes of knowledge as well. Accordingly, the social practice view is receptive to the thesis that performance practices have their own intrinsic values which it may well be important for the school to cultivate.

Finally, the social practice view will be much more receptive than is the aesthetic view to the thesis that the school ought, where possible, to be willing to have different programs for different students. Possibly every high school student should be taught Shakespeare—but then again, maybe not. It is important that the great cultural tradition of a people be handed on from generation to generation, and in my view there is merit in inducting every student into that tradition to some extent. But why not allow the depth of induction to vary greatly from student to student? And why not allow for a much more diversified view of that tradition itself? There has never been, and there will never be, a human life devoid of all music, of all dramatic performance, of all story-telling, of all visual representation, of all rhythmically ordered words. But I think the evidence is pretty clear that for some people, watching the plays of Shakespeare, no matter how good their high school English teacher was in preparing them, is among their least valuable engagements with drama; that listening to the toccatas and fugues of J. S. Bach, no matter how good their music appreciation course was, is among their least valuable engagements with music. So once again, let's honor the diversity.

The social practice view of the nature and significance of the arts invites a radical—and to my mind, exciting—rethinking of school programs in the arts. Rather than elevating aesthetic contemplation of works of high art above all else, the social practice view is much more egalitarian. It opens things up by inviting us to see worth of many different sorts in many different ways of engaging art. The great challenge is in making sensible choices from among the many possibilities. The basic considerations to be used in making the choices are clear enough. Having selected one particular art practice, we ask about its significance in human life. If significance is established, we ask whether formal education in this particular practice is important, or whether informal education is satisfactory. And lastly, if we agree that formal education is important, we ask about the place within the curriculum of formal education in this practice—of whom should it be required, if of any. For example, should we adopt the Orff or Kodaly program for teaching all students to sing and to play some musical instrument?

Though the basic considerations are thus clear enough, how to apply them will often not be clear. Applying them will require sensitive reflective judgment on the part of curriculum committees. The right answer probably will vary from community to community. There will be disagreements and controversies.

Which tells us something about school education. I have argued that in social practices, aims and standards of excellence change over the years, they vary from one person to another, and they are often contested. The sorts of controversies which arise over curriculum and other parts of school education—namely, controversies over goals and criteria for excellence—indicate that school education is itself a social practice. It's the presence of such controversies that indicates that teaching is more than a skill; it's an art. How dull teaching would be if it weren't.

Dr. Robert Wuthnow
Gerhard R. Andlinger
Professor of Social Sciences
Director, Center for the
Study of Religion
Princeton University

Dr. Wuthnow's research focuses on the diverse manifestations of contemporary religion, including its relationship with public policy, the arts, and social services.

He is the author of some twenty books. Articles on his work have appeared in many major newspapers and news magazines, and his research has been the focus of several national television programs.

Dr. Wuthnow is a graduate of the University of Kansas and received his Ph.D. from the University of California, Berkeley.

Robert Wuthnow

Chapter 3

The Fragmenting of America

In the "Antigone," Sophocles warns that "nobody likes the man who brings bad news."[1] But the bad news about social and moral commitments in our society has become so familiar that it is no longer news. One has only to scan the popular press to see how frequently we are reminded that all is not well. Politicians mount character assaults on their opponents. Random violence and road rage make headlines. Parents abuse their children. Couples seem incapable of staying happily married. An article in one newspaper, striving to avoid being purely negative (unsuccessfully, one would have to say), observes that the good thing about the growing numbers of single women having babies is that their children will be spared the pain of their parents getting divorced.

Or consider the letter printed in a Minnesota paper's advice column from a thirty-six-year-old pastor who says he is losing interest in his wife. "I come from a long line of broken commitments," he writes. "My mother married seven times, my father three times, and my grandparents more than once or twice." He wants to know how he can break this pattern and behave more responsibly toward his own family.

Another letter in a different paper carries these poignant lines from a Cleveland Indians fan. "As I grew up—through broken hearts and broken promises, deaths and divorces—I learned, as we all do, that there isn't much in life you can count on." About the only thing he could count on, he said (with marked irony), was the Cleveland Indians.

Broken promises

Problems like this are not exactly new. Anyone with passing knowledge of the past knows that Americans have often broken their promises and fretted about others' breaking theirs. Historians, especially those interested in the religious history of our nation, will be quick to point out that it is characteristic of our culture to acknowledge and, indeed, worry about our shortcomings. The first settlers in Massachusetts and Virginia conceived of their new colonies as communities of people bound to one another and to God in a covenant relationship. They spoke often of themselves as the new Israel, meaning that they were chosen of God and that they had a special mission to fulfill in the New World. But their leaders frequently used the same image to remind them of how often the Israelites of the Bible had failed to live as God expected them to. Brother killed brother. Children disobeyed their parents. People did not respect their leaders. Leaders disobeyed God. Generations wandered in the wilderness. Hopes of a promised land were deferred. Wars and captivity resulted from wickedness in the land.

Throughout our nation's history these images of failure and fragmentation have been replayed. We have been reminded that discord can weaken a nation to the point of it being vulnerable to exploitation by foreign powers. We have warned ourselves, often with less effectiveness than we would like, about the dangers inherent in racial separation and discrimination.[2] We know at some level that we are a nation built on broken promises to the people who occupied the land before it was subjected to European settlement. We know, too, that greed has been a part of American business in the past, just as it is at present.

It is important, therefore, to recognize that the present concern about the breakdown of our society depends only to a certain extent on evidence that social relationships are deteriorating. The worries expressed by journalists and by social scientists, like the laments of a country singer, stem from recognition that broken commitments are an enduring feature of the human condition. They also grow from theological and philosophical understandings that acknowledge the inevitability of human frailty. As one prominent political philosopher remarked when I asked her why her writings about American democracy were so pessimistic: "You can't help being pessimistic," she replied, "if you're an Augustinian like I am."

With those caveats in mind, it is nevertheless important to consider some of what we do know about social relationships. Social scientists earn their keep by keeping track of these things. And there is a wealth of evidence. Some studies are interesting because they show changes over the past few decades in the ways in which Americans actually behave. Others are interesting because they show how we perceive these changes. I want to focus our attention on the following questions: What exactly do we mean by fragmentation? What is causing it? How can it be overcome?

Evidence of fragmentation

Divorce. Divorce is a good place to start. Most people make promises to each other when they get married and these promises are reinforced by certain laws governing spousal rights, parental responsibilities, the sharing of property, and the like. Even though there have always been reasons for some people not to marry or not to stay married, marriage has been regarded as a "social good." It connects individuals and families, gives them emotional and economic support, and provides children with security.

But, as we know, the divorce rate has risen dramatically in recent decades. Specifically, it has risen from approximately one divorce for every four marriages in 1950 to one divorce for every two marriages in the 1990s. Even with this trend leveling out in the past few years, the cumulative impact is that the proportion of divorced Americans is now about four times as high as it was in 1960.[3]

This is not the place to review studies debating the pros and cons of divorce or its impact on spouses and children. Most people who experience divorce eventually remarry, often within a few years, indicating that people continue to value married life—a preference that continues to be expressed overwhelmingly in national polls as well. But the fact of divorce means that growing numbers of

Americans do have as part of their biography the experience of one of their most important social relationships having been broken. The pastor who wrote to the advice columnist is an example of someone who is having difficulty maintaining his own marriage because of his parents' and grandparents' divorces. In interviews I conduct in my own research, I find that a reluctance to trust others is often rooted in the mistrust that people experienced as children as a result of their parents' marital difficulties.

Politics. In a rather different arena of contemporary life, politics is a topic worth considering because candidates routinely make commitments to the electorate during campaigns. Whether the electorate actually expects politicians to keep their promises is a matter of debate, but we would like to think that politicians mean what they say. Frequently we are disappointed. According to a poll taken prior to the impeachment charges brought against President Clinton, for instance, only 43 percent of the American public regarded the President as a man who keeps his promises.[4] We also know that the public's willingness to trust elected officials has deteriorated badly in recent decades. For instance, in 1971 only 18 percent of the public said they had "hardly any" confidence in the people running the executive branch of the federal government. In other words, most people had at least moderate confidence in the government. In 1973, on the eve of Watergate, this figure remained 18 percent. After Watergate, it rose immediately to 42 percent but then fell back to the mid to high 20 percent range during most of the late 1970s and 1980s. As recently as 1991, only 21 percent said they had hardly any confidence in the people running the executive branch of the federal government. Since then, however, the figure has climbed steadily, reaching 42 percent in 1996, its highest level since Watergate.[5]

Of course, confidence and trust may mean different things, and confidence in government often parallels the economy more than anything else. But these figures, combined with the results of other surveys, seem to suggest that a large minority of the American public do not have much faith that our leaders will keep their promises.

This is certainly a different kind of fragmentation than when we talk about divorce. Yet both suggest a fraying of social relationships. We feel alienated, estranged, even angry.

Business. If we move from the political realm to the world of business, the issues are somewhat different. We normally think of business being conducted in terms of self-interested, arms-length contracts rather than on the basis of enduring social commitments. And yet it is clear that trust is an important aspect of business. In his book *Trust* (revealingly subtitled *The Social Virtues and the Creation of Prosperity*), social theorist Francis Fukuyama argues that the United States has until recently been a society that nurtures moderately high levels of trust (for example, higher than Italy or France but not as high as Germany or Japan) and that American business has flourished as a result.[6] Trust makes it easier to organize people into working teams, creates positive expectations about the likelihood of contracts being honored, and reduces risk. Fukuyama also warns that trust may be declining in the United States.

Compared to politicians, business leaders appear to have fared fairly well in the public's view. In 1971, only 15 percent of the public had "hardly any" confidence in the people running America's "major companies," and in 1996 this figure was virtually the same (14 percent). Although mistrust edged up somewhat during economic recessions (in the early 1970s, for example), it never reached the same levels as for politicians.

Still, there are some worrisome signs. In a 1991 survey I conducted among a representative sample of the U.S. labor force, 88 percent responded that "corruption in business" is a serious or an extremely serious problem in our society.[7] Following the much publicized corporate downsizing and outsourcing in the 1990s, large numbers of Americans have also come to believe that companies do not keep their word to their employees. For instance, a 1996 Gallup poll found that 73 percent of the public believe "businesses' commitment to their workers and their communities" currently constitutes a critical or a very serious problem for the country.[8] Another poll, conducted by Daniel Yankelovich in 1997, was perhaps more encouraging, but also suggested that employees have learned to be somewhat wary of their employers' intentions. When asked, "How much do you personally trust your company to keep its promises to you and other employees," 45 percent responded "a lot," 37 percent said "only somewhat," 14 percent said "not at all," and 4 percent said they were unsure.[9]

Besides the question of how much we trust business leaders, another form of fragmentation in business life hits many people much closer to home. This is the fact that most of us are almost completely at the mercy of the market. In one national study I conducted a few years ago, the average American in his or her late forties had already worked in five different lines of work. In the same study, a third were suffering from burnout, and nearly a fourth had worried in the last year about losing their job. People are shunted from job to job because of the changing demands of the labor market. They also migrate. In the last thirty years, we probably have witnessed the largest migration on a global scale in history. Immigration to the United States during this period has been unprecedented. The average American seldom lives at one address for more than five years.

Legal action. Both in business and in personal life, the growing litigiousness of our society is often taken as yet another sign that social relationships are not what they should be. According to a national survey conducted in 1996, one person in ten claims to have sued someone else—meaning, if there was at least one defendant for every plaintiff, that at least 20 percent of the population has been a party in some way to a lawsuit (of course, if divorces were included, the figure would be much higher).[10]

Perhaps a better indicator, at least of trends, is the number of actual cases that the courts process each year. In 1980, U.S. district courts processed approximately 169,000 civil cases. By 1994, that figure had grown to 236,000, an increase of 40 percent in only 14 years. Over the same period, the number of criminal cases increased 61 percent in district courts; the number of cases heard by U.S. courts of appeals grew by 113 percent; and the U.S. Supreme Court's docket climbed 51 percent. The total number of lawyers, incidentally, increased 49 percent during the 1990s, having already risen by 53 percent during the 1980s and by 24 percent during the 1970s.[11]

Communities. Yet another area in which evidence of change can be seen is in our relationships to our communities. Generally we do not speak of promises in this area, but we do use the language of obligation and responsibility. People speak, for example, about ties to their neighbors, about their civic obligations, and about the pride, ownership, and loyalty they may feel toward their community. But there is a widespread perception that community loyalty is breaking down. In my 1991 survey, 76 percent of the labor force said the "breakdown of community" is a serious or an extremely serious problem in our society. There is some basis for this perception. General social survey results show that 72 percent of Americans spent a social evening visiting their neighbors at least once a year in 1974, but this figure declined to 62 percent by 1991; frequent contact (defined by visiting once a month or more) also declined (from 61 percent to 50 percent).[12]

Religion. It is also worth thinking about religion in this context. Etymologically, religion means to bind, and it is for this reason that words such as commitment, devotion, and adherence are so often used in conjunction with religion. Yet the fact that has impressed most observers of American religion in recent years is the extent to which people pick and choose.[13] Fewer than half of all Protestants remain in the denomination in which they were raised, and growing numbers of Protestants and Catholics marry outside their own traditions, as do Christians and Jews. In personal interviews, people speak openly of how they have shopped for different churches, and how they have pieced together their own beliefs from the reading they have done and from conversations with friends. In such interviews, it is not uncommon to find church people who believe in reincarnation, who regularly consult their horoscopes, and who sleep with sacred rocks beside their beds.

In all these areas, then, there is evidence that binding commitments, long-term relationships, and promises may not be as strong as they once were. Other evidence could be cited as well, ranging from the numbers of abused, abandoned, or neglected children in our

society to random shootings in coffee shops and on the nation's
highways, to vivid portrayals of violence and vice on television and
through the Internet. When asked in one recent survey what they
thought of America's "moral and ethical standards," 31 percent of the
public perceived a strong decline, and another 39 percent perceived
a moderate decline, while only 24 percent thought they were holding steady.[14]

Commitment and 'porous relationships'

But we must be careful in how we interpret these developments
and perceptions. Americans are more willing to break or alter their
commitments than they were a few decades ago. But they do try to
make commitments. Indeed, there is powerful evidence that people
are still interested in reaching out to one another and that they are
looking for new ways to relate and to play responsible roles in their
families, at work, and in their communities. It is significant, for
example, that most Americans are still troubled by questions about
commitments. As one survey showed, 77 percent of Americans say
that "failing to follow through on a commitment" would be morally
wrong for them personally, while only 15 percent say this would not
be a moral issue.[15]

In sum, there is ample reason for concern about the quality of
our commitments to one another and to our society, especially as
evidence mounts of growing mistrust, flagging confidence in our
public leaders, and broken promises to our spouses, children, neighbors, and employees. But there is enough evidence as well to indicate
that Americans have not suddenly fallen victim to some fit of ill will
toward one another. We still make commitments, but these commitments are more likely than in the past to be short-term or to become
casualties of changes in our lives.

The word that seems best for describing our current form of
commitments is "porous." Our institutions are porous. They let people, goods, and information flow across their boundaries with relative frequency and ease. A porous neighborhood is one in which

people come and go, move in or move out, work and shop someplace else, and know few of their neighbors very well or for very long. A porous economy moves people around, hires and fires them, uses temporary workers and subcontractors, and encourages mergers and acquisitions. Porous national boundaries are hard to police; tourists and migrant workers come and go. A porous church is one people attend because there's a program for their kids on Sunday or a yoga class on Wednesday night. These kinds of relationships are very different from those of the past. They are not all bad. But we need to understand the reasons why they have become so familiar.

Affluence. The relative affluence of the United States is, ironically, one of the principal reasons why we so often sever our long-term relationships. Perhaps it is counter-intuitive to say so, but long-term relationships are more often born of necessity than of abundance. People are especially likely to keep their promises when they have few other opportunities available. Affluence has given Americans unparalleled opportunities to make, break, and forge new social commitments. I do not mean to suggest that rich people break their promises more often than poor people. By affluence, I mean the general abundance that characterizes our society at the end of the twentieth century relative to that in many other parts of the world and throughout much of history.

Affluence creates opportunities to break ties in a variety of ways. In an isolated mining town, say, in the hills of Kentucky, workers may establish long-term commitments to the mine and to the company store because they have few other options. Were they able to purchase a house somewhere else, or spend a few years getting a better education, they might terminate these commitments and move on to a different job. Similarly, divorce has become much more of an option as a result of women's increased participation in the labor force. Rather than being tied economically to their husbands, women have been better able to earn their own living. At the same time, the fact that women and children suffer financially from divorce continues to mean there are economic costs involved. In other ways, affluence simply gives people access to information: think of the

opportunities that people who can afford to go to college learn about
or, for that matter, the opportunities available to those who can
afford to purchase a home computer and log on to the Internet.

Global markets. The affluence of our society is in turn a function of the dynamic global market in which all Americans are so
deeply involved. This, too, is a reason why our social commitments
have been changing. Companies do not downsize and turn to temporary workers without reason. Part of the reason is to maintain their
competitive edge in world markets. Politicians may be unable to keep
campaign promises because of shifts in the global economy: an unex-
pected increase in the price of Middle Eastern oil or a decision in
Japan to sell off U.S. treasury bonds. Families uproot from their
communities because the breadwinner's company suddenly needs
more personnel in Southeast Asia. Since the revision of immigration
laws in 1965, global markets have also encouraged thousands of families from other countries to migrate to the United States. Even religion is influenced by global markets, as tourism and immigration put
Americans into more frequent contact with Hindus and Buddhists
and Muslims.

Velocity of social transaction. It is a truism to say that markets
seek to expand. They do so in a number of ways: by reaching into
remote corners of the world, by introducing new technologies, and
by drawing people in as consumers. Perhaps more significantly,
though, they also expand by increasing the velocity with which social
transactions occur. A customer who makes a purchase once a week is
more valued than a customer who makes a purchase once a year. This
is one of the reasons why long-term social commitments are increasingly being replaced by short-term commitments. Disposable cameras and disposable diapers are examples of products geared toward
short-term commitments. But these are fairly trivial examples: think
of the money to be made in the real estate market by virtue of the
fact that people buy and sell houses every few years. The situation
would be quite different if people stayed put for a lifetime. Or think
of the thousands of people whose livelihoods depend on the fact that
major presidential campaigns and congressional campaigns happen
as often as they do. We have, in short, developed an economic

system that thrives on a high velocity of social transactions.

Brokering mechanisms. And one of the neglected factors on which all markets depend is what might be called "brokering mechanisms." Let me return to those statistics on lawyers. There would not have been such dramatic increases in the numbers of young people choosing law as a profession in recent decades if lawyers could not find work to do. Lawsuits are easier to file because there are hundreds of thousands of lawyers eager to file them. Divorces are easier, too. More broadly, consider the vast array of occupations that exist primarily to broker some kind of social transaction, whether it be an exchange of goods, or information, or people: stock brokers, travel agents, airlines, therapists, real estate agents, headhunters, temp agencies, just to name a few. Nobody would argue that these brokers are the main reason why we break our social ties more easily than in the past. They smooth the process. They help us slip into and out of our commitments with less difficulty.

Individualism. Markets also generate cultural norms that have a life of their own. Self-interest, greed, consumerism, and advertising are often mentioned. We might also emphasize individualism. I am not inclined to think that Americans are innately any more individualistic, self-interested, or greedy than they were in the past. But there are social pressures that encourage us to be individualistic. I remember a conversation I overheard not long ago among thirteen-year-olds. They were discussing what they believed about God.

The conversation went something like this. "I don't think God should let people suffer," said one.

"I don't think God has anything to do with it," said another.

"Well," said a third, "I don't worry much about suffering or dying because I believe in reincarnation."

Thirteen-year-olds! Why did they think they had a right to an opinion on such matters at all? Because they had been taught from birth to have opinions about everything—and to think that their opinions mattered.

What does this have to do with markets? Markets are places where all that matters are opinions. Of course one should shop for good value, getting the most for one's money. But after that, it is all a matter of taste. Preferences, as economists call them. Thus, people spend a great deal of their time trying to figure out what their preferences are. Our parents and teachers and friends authorize us to do this: "Well, that's your opinion," we say. Or, "In my view, this is what I believe at the moment." And preferences are not always amenable to long-term commitments. We know our preferences are subject to change. They depend on how we feel at the moment. They depend on the experiences and relationships that have shaped us to that point in our lives. And, as our self-concept, interests, or beliefs change, we may feel compelled to move on to new commitments. Thus, it is not uncommon to hear people talk about how they grew away from their spouse, how they switch political parties depending on how they may feel the night before the election, or how they have changed religions in order to gain new insights about themselves.

Population increase. One other factor that bears mentioning is the sheer increase in population. In 1900, a century ago, there were only 75 million people in the United States. By 1950, that number had doubled—to 150 million. It is expected to double again—to 300 million—by the year 2010. And by 2050, it will approach 400 million. These changes, of course, are relatively small by world standards. In just the last two decades, the world's population has grown by nearly 2 billion.

But even in the United States, it is clear that population change is having an effect on the ways in which people behave. Part of the change stems from the fact that the population is becoming more heavily concentrated in certain areas as it grows. When the economy was chiefly agricultural, people spread out on farms and in small towns. At present, more than two-thirds of the population is crowded into metropolitan areas. The result is that most of us live among strangers. Apart from the few people we know in our neighborhoods or at work, we do not know the people we see on the highway or at the supermarket and, as churches become larger, we do not know most of our fellow congregates either.

People behave differently around strangers than they do among close acquaintances. You make promises to people to whom you can be held accountable—people you know, or people who know your friends and who can make trouble for you if you do not keep your promises. It is less common to make promises to strangers. Instead, we rely on brokers to help us negotiate our transactions with strangers—a lawyer, perhaps, or a real estate agent, someone whose training, license, and livelihood help to ensure that a successful transaction will take place.

Then, too, we simply have to engage in a greater variety of relationships when we live in a more densely populated society. In a small town, the grocer may also be the mayor, a neighbor, and a member of one's church. In a city or suburb, these are likely to be different people. And the thing about social relationships is that they increase geometrically, rather than arithmetically—which is at least one of the reasons why lawsuits increase. Suppose you live in a world with only one other person: there are two chances for a lawsuit (you can sue that person, and that person can sue you). But if the world has three people, there are six chances for lawsuits (actually more, if class-action suits are included). In a four-person world, there would be sixteen chances for lawsuits. And so it goes.

Complexity of social institutions

My point is not to trivialize—and certainly not to excuse—the changes we see in our social commitments. But I do think we need to understand the social conditions in which we live. For a whole variety of reasons—economic, cultural, demographic—our social institutions are more complex than they were in the past. Our communities are larger. Many of our organizations, especially government bureaus and international corporations, are larger. We interact with a wider variety of people. We depend on goods and services that are embedded in complex global markets. And we are bombarded with information as a result of television, global satellite networks, cellular telephones, motion pictures, and the Internet. To live in today's world often does require us to be more flexible in our commitments. We do not join the Odd Fellows and spend three nights a week at the lodge for the rest of our lives. Our spouses would not put up with it. Instead, we volunteer for Habitat for Humanity on the occasional Saturday morning when we are not driving our children to soccer practice, staying home for the repairman, going on a business trip, or recuperating from one.

Making choices; ethical reflection

Understanding the sources of our changing contemporary problems should not lead, then, simply to decrying these changes but to seeing the broader issues to which moral and ethical deliberation should be directed. Were the full picture to be considered, the broken relationships we experience in our families and among our business associates would require paying some attention to family-leave policies that make it easier for parents to spend time with their children and with each other. It would require talking about the asymmetric relationships that pit advertising agencies with highly paid professionals against the harried parent who is supposed to police everything his or her children see on television. It would include consideration of business norms that unthinkingly assume the best way to groom corporate executives is to transfer them from one community to another at random intervals.

One thing that seems indisputable about the present situation, however, is that it does require individuals to make an enormous number of decisions about how they wish to lead their lives. Institutional arrangements may make it harder to maintain long-term commitments, but they do not make it impossible. Many people still find it intensely rewarding to stay married, to live at the same address, and to keep their promises to their friends and neighbors. The difficulty is that we are often poorly prepared to think through our options. With nobody looking over our shoulder, it may seem easier to cheat on our expense reports than to file them properly. Indeed, as I found in the research for my book on work and money, tacit norms, rather than thoughtful decisions, often govern such behavior.[16]

The role of stories. The task of ethics is partly to spin webs of meaning in which the implications of alternative choices can be considered. We misinterpret the role of ethics when we regard it strictly as a way of thinking logically about difficult subjects, just as we do if we regard it only as a search for absolute moral principles. When I was studying high school students to see how they learned how to make altruistic choices, I found that they were often motivated by stories. Some of the stories were ones they had read, such as stories about the Good Samaritan or Mother Teresa; others were ones they had created about their own behavior. The stories supplied connective tissue, as it were, between implicit values that they already knew and the concrete situations in which they found themselves. Typically, the stories helped them to make sense of who they were and of why they had made particular choices.[17]

Among adults, stories also provide the key to understanding many of their decisions about working, spending, and getting. In fact, most people work (by their own accounts, at least) not so much just to earn money but so that they can give a legitimate account of themselves: working is a meaningful part of their identity. But, again, the problem is that employers and advertisers know this too. Corporate cultures are replete with myths about caring and warm mom-and-pop relationships or about upward mobility and prestige. Advertisers spin visual narratives about relationships between new automobiles and the open road, luxury, power, and sex. It is simply a novel idea to many people to think that there may be alternative stories in which to think about their lives.

The same point can also be made about bringing ethics to bear on public policy. Recent studies show the great extent to which policymakers rely on familiar scripts to tell them what to do. French and British railways developed quite differently in the nineteenth century, for example, primarily because officials had different precedents in their minds that precluded them from thinking in new ways.[18] Conversely, as a lobbyist confided to me on one occasion, one of the most effective ways of changing policymakers' minds is to tell them stories that illustrate a new way of thinking.

In themselves, stories are inevitably limited. They need to be reinforced through reflection and criticism; otherwise, they become self-legitimating. Among the teenagers I studied, the easiest stories to tell about helping others were that it was required by one's school or that it would look good on one's college application. These stories didn't require much thought. Nor did they link very deeply to a student's character. The more effective community service programs included opportunities for students to write journal entries about their experiences and then to discuss these narratives with the guidance of a teacher or sponsor. Those kinds of reflective experiences changed the way students thought about themselves. They came to think of themselves as caring people, not simply as someone fulfilling a community service requirement. And, having developed a new identity, they also saw more possibilities for service in the future. They imagined themselves doing volunteer work or going into the helping professions. Similarly, among adults, it does make a difference for people to take classes in business ethics, to participate in workshops or task forces concerned with ethical issues, or to take part in voluntary support groups.

Economic justice. Besides storytelling, ethical reflection also requires paying attention to values that may run counter to the pleasure-maximizing norms that so often govern the marketplace. Among these, economic justice is perhaps the most important. As we know, the economic expansion that has taken place in the 1980s and 1990s has not benefited everyone equally. At one extreme, more and more of the nation's wealth is concentrated among the very few at the top. At the other extreme, life has become much harder for many at the bottom. Incomes have shrunk, union membership has declined, jobs in manufacturing have been replaced by lower-paying jobs in fast-food and other unskilled service occupations, benefits and job security have diminished. Moreover, a growing share of the poor are children or are among the elderly, and in many cities, the poor are more geographically concentrated than in the past.

All this means that substantial numbers of Americans are in danger of simply falling through the cracks as social institutions become more porous. Indeed, some studies show that the effects of children being raised by one rather than by two parents are inconsiderable in upper-income groups but become significantly negative among the poor. Other research suggests that much of the decline in voter registration, voter turnout, civic participation, and membership in community organizations has been among the disadvantaged. Why? Middle- and upper-income people can afford to seek alternatives: for-profit nursery schools, professional advice, and new kinds of civic groups. In contrast, lower-income people may live in neighborhoods where there are no longer organizations in which to participate, and their friends and families may be too strapped to provide significant assistance. Part of any discussion of the ethics of broken commitments, therefore, must focus on ways in which to reinvigorate commitments to the disadvantaged.

The role of religion. Ethical reflection generally does not happen spontaneously. It has to be planned and organized. As my comments about teenagers suggest, schools and community service programs can be one of these places. Among adults, continuing education programs and volunteer centers can serve a similar function. But we also need to focus especially on the churches. With some 350,000 local congregations and nearly two-thirds of the public on their membership rolls, the churches can make a powerful difference.

One role that churches and other religious organizations can play is to provide places for thoughtful, faith-informed ethical reflection. Increasingly, congregations are making use of small groups to nurture such reflection. Small groups can provide alternatives—countercultures—to the norms of the workplace and the marketplace. Among peers, people can tell their stories and listen to the stories of others. By getting to know one another, they can build some of the trust that is lacking in the wider society and they can overcome the strong social taboos that inhibit people from talking about their personal finances.

Small groups are a part of most congregations' efforts to build "community" among their members. The idea of community is itself an attractive role for the churches to fulfill. Community is part of what people long for when they think about the "old days" when neighbors helped neighbors and when honest men and women kept their word. Congregations can, in this sense, be a corrective to the fragmentation that is taking place in the wider society.

But clergy and lay leaders are likely to be disappointed if they perceive their congregations only as communities. Despite the popularity of talk about "community" in churches, religious organizations are increasingly having to adapt to the more complex circumstances of the wider society as well. In fact, many churches now serve mainly as brokers. Church staff take phone calls, answer questions, and direct people to various services and opportunities for service within the congregation or in the wider community. Members move in to and out of small groups and other activities, depending on their needs and interests of the moment. The flexibility of these arrangements works well in many large suburban churches. But it also suggests a need for conscious attention to be devoted to spiritual and ethical formation.

Another role that religious organizations can play is to provide damage control. As government programs for the needy have been scaled back, congregations are being asked to play more of a role in caring for the disadvantaged. Soup kitchens are perhaps the clearest example, but increasingly congregations are experimenting with more creative alternatives as well. Some are forming coalitions with other congregations. Others are initiating nonprofit social service agencies. Still others are cooperating with government and business to plan large-scale community initiatives such as housing and urban redevelopment. There is also an opportunity for congregations to do more to minister to middle-class victims of broken commitments. Support groups for alcoholics and members of dysfunctional families, job-retraining programs, and counseling centers are among the responses to these opportunities.

Spiritual discipline. The final role I want to mention is that of nurturing spiritual discipline. Although social support is always needed, it is often too easy to rely on the congregation or on friends and family to make the hard decisions in life. The freedom that our society provides means that we often need to make these hard decisions in our own way. Yet these decisions also need to be informed by spiritual and ethical reflection. Perhaps it is time for the churches to rediscover the wisdom of the contemplative life and of similar spiritual disciplines. People who have taken responsibility to cultivate their spiritual life by praying, meditating, and worshiping on a daily basis routinely say that their lives—including their commitments—have been transformed.

Robert Wuthnow

Chapter 4

Teaching Forgiveness

A fragmented society generates many situations in which people feel betrayed. Confusion, frustration, and disappointment have become common ways to describe our social relationships. Spouses who experience divorce illustrate one of these situations. The fact that so many marriages end in divorce may be of some comfort to them. At least they know divorce is not that unusual. Yet we know that divorce is frequently accompanied by feelings of betrayal and resentment. People feel they have failed themselves or their spouses, or they feel angry at their spouse's failure. They find it hard to forgive themselves or their spouse. Children of divorced parents often struggle with finding a way to forgive their parents.

Newspapers are filled with stories about people who have become so frustrated with their relationships that they have, as it were, gone over the edge: the now-too-familiar stories of laid-off employees who murder their employer or fellow employees; the alienated child who plots revenge against classmates and teachers; and the student who takes revenge by shooting classmates and teachers.

Some of these tragic events are aggravated by the fragmented conditions of our society. Being laid off is a common occurrence in a society that relies solely on market relations to determine employment patterns. Students taking revenge at school may be acting out anger fomented by parents' divorce, abusive parents, or even overcrowded classrooms.

The typical response in these situations is to call for stiffer laws with harsher penalties. With good reason, we focus on questions of prevention and restitution. But there is that troubling clause in the Lord's Prayer: "Forgive us our trespasses as we forgive those who trespass against us." Some observers argue that we could benefit by paying more attention to forgiveness. In this view, the ill effects of a fragmented society are not restricted to the fact that people get divorced or lose their jobs. The negative consequences of these experiences are compounded by the fact that people respond by breaking other relationships or by drowning in guilt or anger. Forgiveness could heal these problems. It might not overcome the problems of fragmentation, but it could help us move past broken relationships to lead more productive lives.

I want to consider what we know about forgiveness. What exactly is it? How do people think about it? What experiences prompt it or make it difficult? Can it be nurtured and learned? What should churches be doing to encourage it? Is it an appropriate subject for schools? It will be helpful to consider some examples and some evidence. I will be drawing on a major study in which I am presently engaged. But let me start with an example from my own experience.

A personal story

The date is sometime in the early 1960s. The place is a small town in Kansas. My hometown. I am in junior high. We were in the process of moving from the farm, where I had been raised, to the town some twelve miles away where my mother was now teaching and where I went to school. While I waited at the library for my mother to finish work, my father stopped at the filling station for gas and to catch up with the neighborhood gossip. As we drove home to our farm that evening, my father announced that our neighbor, Mr. Stafford, had been shot. At least that was the gossip at the filling station. He apparently was not dead but had been rushed to the hospital in Wichita in serious condition. The Kansas Bureau of Investigation had been brought in, but the perpetrators were still at large.

I remember that evening as vividly as if it were yesterday. This was only a year after the brutal murders of all five members of the Herbert Clutter family in western Kansas—the slayings that Truman Capote made famous in his book *In Cold Blood*. People in our farming community were still edgy. As we returned to our farm that evening, we imagined it as a likely place for killers to be hiding. We were the Staffords' closest neighbors. Looking across the farm yard at our barn, we knew someone could easily take refuge there. But we decided to leave well enough alone. The house was a different matter. My parents searched the house from top to bottom before we felt safe enough to go to bed.

A day or two later, we learned that the police had arrested Danny Smith and charged him with attempted murder. Danny Smith was in eighth grade. He lived on a farm a mile to the south. Various versions of the story were heard at the filling station, but the one that seems closest to the truth is as follows:

Mr. Stafford and his wife were an elderly couple who had moved to the community a few years before because of a part-time job Mr. Stafford had taken checking a gas pipeline that ran through the area. He had hired Danny Smith to do some yard work for him and had befriended him. But tools and household items occasionally seemed to be missing. One day Mr. Stafford confronted Danny, accusing him of stealing, and an angry exchange ensued. That evening Danny quietly took his father's hunting rifle, walked the mile to Mr. Stafford's house, waited until he appeared at the window, and pulled the trigger.

The outcome was not as bad as it could have been. But two lives were very nearly destroyed. The bullet entered Mr. Stafford's left eye, permanently blinding him, and lodged in his brain. After a year of recovery, the Staffords moved to Oklahoma. Danny was convicted and spent a number of years in prison. Nobody in the community knows what has become of him.

Could an incident like this have been prevented? Perfect hindsight points to the problem of hunting rifles not being kept in locked places. It points to family dynamics (Danny's older brother was a model student who received more praise from his parents than

Danny did). Perhaps Mr. Stafford's accusation was unwarranted, overly harsh, or at least ill-timed. The episode certainly raises questions about forgiveness. What would it have taken for the parties involved to forgive each other or themselves?

Tragedies involving crime, violence, or both are rare, but not that rare. The body of a man in his early thirties who was a popular high school teacher is found stuffed in the closet of a male prostitute. A teenage boy who has been expelled for using drugs waits every afternoon at an appropriate distance down the street from the high school to meet his former classmates and supply them with drugs. A teenage girl who has recently received her driver's license takes a curve too fast and, when the car careens into a ditch, her two friends in the back seat are killed. These are true stories that our daughter came home with when she was in high school.

Ironically, our institutions are sometimes better equipped to deal with extreme tragedies than with ordinary wear and tear in our relationships. Social workers, school psychologists, judges, wardens, and clergy are called into action for the big events. But it is the smaller, less visible strains that need attention. These are more common. They are the result of living in an increasingly fragmented society.

A national research project on forgiveness

I am currently engaged in a national research project on forgiveness. With funding from the John Templeton Foundation, we are attempting to learn more about how people experience forgiveness and the circumstances that facilitate or impede it. In a preliminary phase of the research, we interviewed approximately one hundred people about a wide variety of personal issues, commitments, and spiritual and religious activities. These interviews included a brief section on forgiveness. Then we developed a more extensive set of questions about forgiveness and recruited several dozen people to be interviewed using these questions. And we conducted a national survey.

People vary considerably in how much they have had to deal with forgiveness. In our first round of interviews, the hundred people we talked to divided about equally into two categories. The first category denied that forgiving others or forgiving themselves had ever been much of an issue for them. Some admitted they had never really been in a situation that called for forgiveness. Their lives had apparently been free of conflict. Most in this category said they had experienced conflict, but their response was just to forgive and forget. The most typical response in this category was simply, "No, I'm not the type of person to hold a grudge." For these people, forgiveness apparently was so easy or natural that they didn't have to think much about it. And for this reason they were unable to help us much in trying to learn more about it. The other half, though, told stories that showed the difficulties and complexities involved in forgiveness.

Not surprisingly, the relationships that most frequently evoke concerns about forgiveness are the relationships that make up our ordinary daily lives. Most of them are with family members or with people at work (or, in the case of students, at school). Divorce is frequently mentioned. People struggle to forgive their spouse or to overcome their own feelings of failure. Adults frequently mention being sexually abused or abused in other physical ways by their parents. Sometimes the problem involves sibling rivalry or financial dealings with relatives. In the workplace, problems typically involve losing one's job, having one's job threatened, or being passed over for a promotion. The seemingly petty irritants of work life also abound. These include being gossiped about, having one's ideas stolen, and being subjected to verbal abuse.

Understanding forgiveness

After poring over such stories and trying to figure out what forgiveness was, I went back to some of the popular books that have been written about forgiveness. Nearly every popular television preacher and lecture-circuit psychologist has written a book about forgiveness. But the more I read, the more I became convinced that there is a disjuncture between the way these experts talk about forgiveness and the way people actually experience it. In fact, there seem to be several common ways in which the expert literature generates *misunderstanding* about forgiveness.

I have already alluded to one of these misunderstandings: that forgiveness is an exceptional activity that arises under extremely unusual circumstances. A recent example of this view was a story on a popular television documentary program about a woman who publicly forgave a man who had been convicted of murdering her husband. The news media love such stories because they tug at people's heartstrings. In reality, forgiveness usually happens in ordinary situations, if it happens at all.

A second misunderstanding is that forgiveness is best understood as pardoning someone's wrongdoing. This view comes from focusing too narrowly or too literally on the definition of the word itself. If one looks up "forgive" in *Webster's New World Dictionary*, one sees it defined as "to give up resentment against or the desire to punish; stop being angry with; pardon." And secondary meanings include giving up "all claim to punish or exact penalty for (an offense)" and canceling or remitting a debt. The problem with this view is that forgiveness is often required in situations where wrongdoing is ambiguous. People find it difficult to know exactly if someone has violated a rule. They are caught up in wondering exactly how they should feel and respond.

Another common misunderstanding is that forgiveness is a form of altruism. To be altruistic means doing something purely for the benefit of someone else with no regard to seeking personal gain. Thought of in this way, forgiveness implies that there is nothing in the deal for me. But things are seldom this simple. Most people who have struggled with forgiveness acknowledge that there is something in it for them too. Overcoming guilt or restoring a friendship benefits the forgiver as well as the forgiven.

A somewhat more subtle misunderstanding is the idea that forgiveness involves a transaction between two people. The stereotypic example is someone going to the offending party, talking frankly with them, and either apologizing or evoking an apology. But we do live in a society of strangers. The motorist who cuts us off in traffic makes us seethe, and yet there is no way we can track down that person and make them apologize. A lot of forgiveness involves working through our own feelings. And, importantly, that may result from talking to third parties rather than to the offending party.

A related misunderstanding is the idea that forgiveness is a distinct activity that can be separated from the rest of one's life. Sometimes the experts treat it as if it were an illness: with seven easy steps, the problem can be cured. The advice focuses on getting in touch with one's feelings about the problem and then confronting the other person about it. But for most people, it is more complex. The problem sometimes shatters their entire image of themselves. Or they have to work around it by finding different ways to renew a relationship with someone.

Much of the expert advice emphasizes willpower and moral fortitude. The biggest problem is getting up the courage to confront someone. Or the broader need for forgiveness results from some moral failing in our society. People are said to be too proud or selfish, or they haven't been taught the right moral principles. All this may be true, but people who effectively engage in forgiveness seldom do it just by cranking up their moral resolve. They do it with a lot of help from their friends. They talk it out, seek advice, and secure support.

These observations suggest that forgiveness may be problematic for many people simply because they don't understand it. As children, they may have been admonished "to forgive and forget," "not carry a grudge," or "go say you're sorry," and from these admonitions came to think of forgiveness as being trivial or easily accomplished. When adult life puts them in more difficult situations, these simple admonitions are no longer adequate.

We have also been influenced by the heroic portrayals of forgiveness in the movie *Dead Man Walking* or in similarly moving stories of bereaved parents and friends forgiving Timothy McVeigh for the Oklahoma City bombing. These stories make us think forgiveness is fine for saints, but impossible for ordinary people. In instances of lawbreaking or misconduct by public officials, we may learn that forgiveness is foolhardy. The emphasis in such instances is more likely to be on punishment and upholding the law. Forgiveness may seem to condone wrongful behavior.

Who should teach forgiveness?

If forgiveness is a difficult, easily misunderstood subject, it can only be made a more effective part of our lives through deliberate effort. It does not seem to come naturally. It needs to be taught and learned. But who should teach it?

Churches. For most Americans, forgiveness has religious connotations. In our interviews, many people talked about feeling that they had failed God when they hurt someone or felt angry toward someone. They talked about asking God to forgive them. And they often admitted that it was easier to seek God's forgiveness than someone else's forgiveness. These comments pointed toward the churches as the appropriate place for teaching forgiveness.

People do, in fact, learn about forgiveness by hearing sermons, attending Sunday school classes, and talking to their pastors. My research has focused especially on the role of small groups in churches, such as Bible studies and prayer fellowships. These and other small groups have become increasingly popular in recent years. Between 35 percent and 40 percent of adult Americans regularly attend some kind of small supportive group, and two-thirds of these groups are sponsored by churches. The members of these groups are often exposed to discussions about forgiveness. They sometimes study biblical lessons that point to the need for forgiveness. They frequently discuss personal problems and pray about these problems. Approximately two-thirds of all group members report that they have been enabled to forgive someone as a result of being in their group. About two-thirds also say the group has helped them forgive themselves.

Parents. But churches should not be the only places where forgiveness is discussed. A third of all Americans do not belong to any church, and as many as three-fourths do not worship or attend services on a regular basis. Moreover, many people compartmentalize their lives. So talking about forgiveness at church may have little spillover to what they do at work or at home during the week. In our interviews, we found that some of the best teaching about forgiveness still happened in the home. Good parents, especially those who had good parents, took time to talk with their children about forgiveness. Small tiffs or even episodes of petty theft or revenge became times for parental guidance. People also reported learning about forgiveness by attending counseling sessions, taking part in group therapy or book discussion clubs, and talking with friends.

Schools. The role of schools is clearly more difficult. If forgiveness is defined as a religious topic, then school officials may deem it outside their purview. But when forgiveness is understood as a more general feature of group dynamics and human relations, then it is harder to say it has no place in the classroom. In our interviews we found a few instances of schools making an important difference in people's understanding of forgiveness. Teachers sometimes served as powerful role models. They may have confessed some wrongdoing to their students and asked forgiveness. We also found several examples of people remembering special events, such as an assembly speaker who had been on drugs and sought forgiveness for his offenses, or a peer counseling session involving anger and reconciliation. But these examples were fairly uncommon.

Community organizations. If the schools were to do more to promote forgiveness, one strategy that might prove effective would be the one we found in a community study in Pennsylvania. This study focused on the ways in which community organizations are adapting to the increasingly porous institutions in their area, including declining participation in traditional service clubs (such as Rotary and Kiwanis), diminishing interest in the PTA, growing ethnic diversity, population growth, and a shifting economic base.

The general finding was that new community organizations were springing up. These new organizations were more loosely structured and loosely connected than older ones. They used hotlines and the Internet, and they worked by developing strategic networks with other organizations, including the schools and churches.

In one school in a metropolitan area of Pennsylvania, an effective violence prevention network had emerged. It came about when a school principal phoned the human services department following an incident of racial violence at the school. A human services worker called several of her friends and formed a new voluntary organization. That organization has taken the initiative to bring assembly speakers to the schools and has prepared informational packets. This information addresses a range of issues, including anger, resentment, reconciliation, and forgiveness.

In an adjacent county, an equally interesting program had developed. This was a peer mediation project in the schools themselves. The leader had become interested in peace-making because of a study group at her church. After years of thinking about international peace, she realized there was much to do in her own community. She set up a nonprofit organization for herself, got a grant from the state, and sold the program to the school board. It mostly involved working individually with students and with pairs of students who had gotten into trouble. Forgiveness was often an important part of her work.

The other possibility for encouraging more learning about forgiveness in schools is suggested by the research I did a few years ago on community service and volunteering among high school students. The importance of structured activities and of times for reflection that emerged in that research has implications for teaching forgiveness.

Altruistic behavior was more effectively learned when students came to see it as part of their relations to institutions, rather than viewing it only as engaging in random acts of kindness. They realized they could serve others by preparing for a career or by participating in a service club at school. Many times, they were put in situations where they saw needs for the first time and had to reflect on an appropriate response.

Forgiveness may be harder to learn than compassion, but it can probably be learned in the same contexts. Service learning that puts students in new settings may be valuable. Students may gain a better understanding of why some people are angry and resentful. Students who take part in peer leadership programs or service clubs also learn that human nature is flawed. As some of our adult interviewees observed, they had to do a lot of repair work to keep on good terms with other volunteers.

What should be taught?

We come then to the question of what should be taught about forgiveness. The answer is both general and specific. The general answer is that forgiveness needs to be taught in a way that encourages people to practice it. The specific answer involves insights that work only if people are already oriented positively toward the value of practicing forgiveness.

By practice, I am referring to a cluster of ideas that have become prominent in scholarly discussions over the past decade about moral practice and spiritual practice. The essential idea is that people learn not so much by absorbing knowledge cognitively but by engaging in activities that become habitual parts of their behavior. Learning to play the piano is a fitting example. Although it may be possible to learn certain things about piano through reading, the ability to play the piano basically requires practice.

In other realms, practices are said to be clusters of activities that require following certain rules in order to gain skill, but practices also require some creativity, and they result in character being developed as one pursues them over long periods of time. Artists I have interviewed, for example, talk frequently about the courage and discipline it takes to become skilled at painting or sculpture, and they describe other virtues such as learning how to take risks or learning to forgive themselves when they fall short of their expectations. Most any practice that a person pursues seriously becomes a significant part of that person's identity. Being an artist comes to define who one is. Engaging in spiritual practices, such as prayer and meditation, over long periods of time also shapes one's identity.

Conceived of as a practice, forgiveness takes on characteristics that make it different from the popularized misunderstandings mentioned earlier. It is not a special skill that one pulls out on special occasions, but a way of life. It may include, but is not limited to, talking with someone about a particular grievance or event. Rather, it involves all of one's relationships and, on special occasions, requires creativity in finding ways to mend broken relationships.

Because of the ambiguity of wrongdoing, forgiveness is one of those practices that we come to know and apply at an intuitive level. Reasoning may well be involved. But people who have learned over the years to be forgiving people cannot always tell why one course of action seemed right in one situation and not in another. Forgiveness has become natural enough to them that they don't have to think about it, just as swimming is natural to a fish.

Forgiveness, nevertheless, continues to require some moral commitment. Unlike a fish, people generally make a conscious effort to swim, and they have to remind themselves periodically of the importance of forgiving; otherwise, their commitment will diminish. This is why most practices, even those that require a lot of individual training, are helped by being around other people. These peers not only remind one that the practice is rewarding but also provide encouragement.

The specific insights that may be helpful in learning how to practice forgiveness are best communicated through the words of some of the people we interviewed. Practices are so deeply embedded in individual lives that they are best learned by having role models, mentors, and by listening to stories about the real-life struggles of these mentors. Here is one example.

Helen Saxman is a third-grade teacher in her early forties, married, and the mother of two teenagers. A life-long Presbyterian, her father was a pastor, as is her husband. As a child, she thought it was nice being the minister's daughter because everyone in the congregation paid her special attention. By the time she was a teenager, things had changed. She recalls hating the double life she was leading: pretending to have all the answers in public, but privately entertaining doubts and having questions about her faith that she dared not reveal to anyone. She nevertheless stayed involved.

Soon after college, she married a man who was just graduating from seminary, and together they moved to a new community where his first pastorate was a small church needing to be revitalized with strong leadership from the pulpit. They succeeded and, after five years, her husband was called as head pastor of a much larger church. Helen was happy to move because the new church offered a better Sunday school program for their children and richer opportunities for worship, service, and fellowship. She continued to teach at a local elementary school while devoting most of her spare time to activities at the church. There were the usual squabbles and petty grievances, but relationships at the church were generally positive.

They had been at this church about a decade when the music director started agitating for a higher salary and even threatened to leave. Helen's husband opposed the raise because he felt it was excessive and violated the congregation's expectations about how its giving would be used. The personnel committee eventually approved the music director's request and she stayed. But her relations with Helen's husband were strained and steadily deteriorated over the next several years. The music program was popular among the congregates, so the director continued to receive the congregation's support, but she felt betrayed by Helen's husband. He in turn found it increasingly difficult to work with her but was unable to persuade leaders of the congregation to ask her to leave. Rumors and misgivings circulated to the point that the matter was taken to a higher committee at the Presbytery level. Helen's husband was asked to resign.

Several years have passed, and Helen is still angry and hurt by the incident. While it was unfolding, she tried to keep an open mind and provide counsel to her husband about how best to achieve reconciliation with the music director. But the conflict brought back memories of similar troubles in the church of her childhood. She was never sure how to respond then and she is unsure how to respond now. She says, "I really have been an innocent, truly an innocent, in something like this where I've been really hurt and my family's been hurt. I haven't been able to get to the point of forgiveness. It's more like I'm trying to hold back from murdering them, or saying something, or murdering their spirit at least."

I will consider some of her insights about forgiveness in a moment, but we can benefit from introducing a second case as well. Like Helen Saxman, Charlie Brock has been troubled lately about a relationship that has gone sour. He is in his early fifties, a civil engineer who works for the Ohio Department of Transportation. When Charlie was a child, growing up on a farm in southern Illinois, his parents taught him "all the traditional Christian values," including honesty, frugality, and getting along with their neighbors. The Brocks were Methodists, as were many of the other farmers in their community, and Charlie went faithfully to Sunday school and worship services at the local Methodist church. Looking back on it, he thinks he absorbed the church's values with few questions because the people avoided being "preachy," choosing instead to show by example what it meant to be a Christian.

Forgiving and being forgiven have always been central to his understanding of what it means to be a Christian. Reflecting on how he and his two siblings were raised, he observes, "We knew that if we did wrong, we should 'fess up and face the music, or whatever it was we had done wrong. But we also knew that once we had dealt with the issue, that we were forgiven, and it was behind us. And it wasn't thrown in our faces again, either, so it really was a Christ-like forgiveness. That was very clear to us."

As an adult, he tries to emulate this understanding of forgiveness in his dealings with others. The relationship that has gone sour is an example. It is with a coworker. He describes her as "very loud and domineering" and suggests that both her personality and the usual tensions in the workplace have made it increasingly difficult to get along with her. Even the slightest miscue on his part can rankle her, and then she may subject him to a barrage of jibes for weeks on end. When this happens, it takes all the patience he can muster to relate to her as he thinks a Christian should.

Both Helen and Charlie have learned that forgiveness is required in situations where feelings and relationships are strained, even though laws haven't been violated or violence committed. Helen wants to blame the music director for overt wrongdoing. For instance, she believes the music director lied about having a more lucrative offer from another church and thinks the music director intentionally spread false rumors about Helen's husband to get him fired. But another part of her believes the incident resulted from people simply making errors of judgment. Her comment about church people being needy is particularly revealing. If everyone has needs that lead them to behave in somewhat selfish or irrational ways, then it is difficult to think about actually pardoning them. Phrases such as "working through my anger" or "learning to get on with life" come closer to what she means when she talks about forgiveness.

Charlie Brock's relationship suggests the subtlety with which forgiveness must be understood as well. He mentions the relationship as an illustration of how his faith influences his behavior, and he brings it up again in talking about forgiveness. Yet he recognizes that a narrow definition of forgiveness does not apply because the woman hasn't done anything overtly wrong. It is rather her personality, her abrasive style of relating to people, and her penchant for retaliation that bothers him. "It's not like she does things that I really have to forgive her for," he muses, "but just the way she operates is totally foreign to me." He says it takes "understanding" to get along with her, and he implies that he feels guilty enough when he thinks ill of her that he has to seek forgiveness for his own feelings.

Just as people may play the piano for their own enjoyment, both Helen and Charlie acknowledge that the practice of forgiveness benefits them personally. Helen acknowledges that learning how to forgive the music director is turning out to be an experience of personal growth. "I've been dealing with this in therapy because I think at the bottom of all of this are things that I need to understand about myself. I'm finding that the reasons why these things are so volatile for me have to do with things that have been happening to me since I was really little and the way I've reacted to them."

She also believes God is using this experience to help her grow spiritually. "God is our refuge and our strength. It's the tough times that make us grow."

Charlie's story comes closer to suggesting that forgiveness may have an altruistic component. At least he feels he is going the extra mile in keeping peace with his coworker. Yet he recognizes that his own job performance depends on having good relations with fellow employees. Like Helen Saxman, he also regards trials like this as a way that God may be trying to strengthen his faith.

One of the clearest insights that both provide is the idea that forgiveness often requires a fundamental shift of perspective or reevaluation of one's own behavior. Helen Saxman's experience is interesting in this regard. An outside observer might argue that the incident would have had a happier ending if Helen's husband and the music director had been able to confront each other, apologize, and ask each other for forgiveness. One might even conclude that the matter will never be fully resolved until a meeting like this takes place. To draw such a conclusion, however, overlooks the circumstances that make such a meeting unlikely. By the time Helen's husband and the music director were at a point where a meeting of this kind might have taken place, they were living thousands of miles apart. Both had taken new jobs that by most accounts were making even better use of their respective talents. More to the point, it must be understood that Helen herself was never a direct party to the conflict. She is an aggrieved party, but knows it would be awkward to meet with the music director while remaining loyal to her husband's side of the conflict. She believes the most realistic resolution of the incident will come about by dealing with her own emotions.

If Helen Saxman's episode were a discrete experience, she might at some point say to herself, if not to the music director, "All right, this has gone on long enough, I forgive you and promise to forget all about it." But her episode is so interwoven with her entire spiritual biography that much more is taking place as she tries to work through it. The experience has forced her to revisit old wounds half forgotten from childhood and, in the process, to relive some of the doubts she has had about her faith. For instance, she has been thinking lately about what it means for God to forgive people and whether she fully understands the Christian doctrine of atonement. She is also coming to terms with feelings about herself, especially the idea that she may have learned to acquiesce too easily with other's opinions rather than standing up for what she thinks is right. The episode is requiring her to ponder how much she should trust other people. And she realizes it will take effort to grow spiritually before she can put this episode behind her.

Charlie Brock's relationship with his coworker isn't a one-shot experience either. He expects to keep interacting with her and hopes to keep peace. Forgiveness blends imperceptibly with simply trying to be nice ("biting my tongue sometimes") and with maintaining an image he has of himself as someone who is generally "nonjudgmental." He doesn't bracket forgiveness from the rest of his faith, his values, or his personality. His conscience is easily pricked if he treats someone badly or inadvertently accepts too much change at the supermarket. On such occasions, he is tacitly aware that God's forgiveness in Christ makes him acceptable to God despite his mistakes. And he responds, not by running to the other person and asking them to pardon him, but by rectifying the problem if he can or by being more careful the next time.

Helen Saxman made up her mind time and time again during the conflict between her husband and the music director that she would simply forgive and forget. A lifetime of instruction in Presbyterian churches had taught her that willpower was important. Yet it wasn't willpower that eventually put her on the path to being able to forgive. It was participating in a group concerned with deepening her devotional life—indeed, participating in several groups, finding them less helpful than she had hoped, and then working with a spiritual director who gradually showed her the value of prayer and meditation.

On one occasion during her daily Bible reading and prayer, Helen was reflecting on the story about Jesus being betrayed by his disciples in the Garden of Gethsemane. She had read the story many times before, but had never been able to relate to it, other than to understand its place in the story of the crucifixion and resurrection. Her spiritual director, however, had encouraged her to take an imaginative role, putting herself in the stories she was reading. When Helen did this, she suddenly saw the connection between Jesus' betrayal and her own sense of having been betrayed by the people at her husband's church. Seeing this connection helped her understand the depths of her own anger. She realizes more clearly now that she will have to work through this anger before she can forgive.

When Charlie Brock is having to bite his tongue at work, it sometimes feels to him like willpower is all that matters. Yet when he reflects on these times, he realizes that his response is conditioned by the fact that he regularly attends church where he hears sermons on forgiveness and encounters people who share his basic values. "It is a nice community feeling. I feel more comfortable with people in the church setting than I do with some of the people I work with. I'm more open with people there and I know that they're more accepting, and so I feel more accepted there, and I feel more accepting within the church community." This acceptance gives him strength to withstand the more difficult relationships he encounters at work.

Helen Saxman's story shows the limitations of trying to reduce forgiveness to some simplistic formula. She is having to confront troubling issues from her childhood, making sense of herself before she can figure out what it truly means to forgive. She understands the church's teachings about forgiveness well enough to know intellectually that they are true, yet it has only been through the story of Jesus' life that she has been able to grasp these teachings. "I can appreciate and value the kind of person Jesus was at this point in my life, where I never could before. I can now look at someone and not say, 'Gosh, you're a jerk. Boy, I really can't stand you.' I can think, 'What's been your journey? What's led you to this place? If you've said this to me or you've done this to me, what's behind that and what's my response going to be to that?' I can still hate the things that they do to me, but there's something beyond that. And when I look at Jesus Christ, there's this knowledge of this person who certainly led a life of integrity but also one of love."

Similarly, Charlie Brock says forgiveness is part of a larger lifestyle that he describes as one of caring, love, and understanding. He probably would argue that these values—in the abstract—are worth following in all times and places. But he doesn't understand them in the abstract. He understands them by reflecting on personal experiences and through the stories he can tell about his experiences. One of these stories is about the love Jesus demonstrated when he died on the cross. Charlie learned this story when he was a child. Other stories emphasize small kindnesses he has experienced at church or within his family. Without these stories, he would have no way of describing what forgiveness is.

Neither of these people has a secret formula for forgiveness. But both have come to understand its importance. Their lives are better as a result. By refusing to run away from their strained relationships, they have experienced personal growth. Forgiveness alone will not overcome the fragmentation of our society. But fragmentation would leave us with fewer scars if we were better able to forgive.

Maribeth VanderWeele
Inspector General
Chicago Public Schools

After graduating from Wheaton College in Illinois and working as a reporter for a suburban Chicago daily newspaper, Ms. VanderWeele served as education writer for the *Chicago Sun-Times.*

In 1995 she became Chief of Investigations for Chicago Public Schools, and in 1998 Mayor Richard Daley appointed her Inspector General, charging her with investigating fraud, waste, and mismanagement in all facets of the nation's third largest school system.

Her book *Reclaiming Our Schools: The Struggle for Chicago School Reform* has served as a road map for the reform movement now under way.

Maribeth VanderWeele

Chapter 5

Surviving Bureaucracy

In the early 1900s, a young Yale University graduate named Robert Moses had dreams for New York State. Where others saw riverfronts filled with garbage, he saw beaches. Where others viewed slums, he envisioned highways. When others shook their heads at the corrupt government of New York's Tammany Hall, the young reformer dreamed of a way to eliminate political influence, particularly in hiring.

In 1914, Robert Moses found his chance. He won the opportunity to develop a civil service code. He built an elaborate system of tests in hiring that he knew would end the rampant corruption in New York bureaucracy. Idealistic and optimistic, he unveiled the project. Thousands of workers protested. In the end, what little progress Robert Moses made over four years was disassembled. He was fired, crushed by Tammany Hall, as Robert Caro recounts in his book *The Power Broker: Robert Moses and the Fall of New York.*

A lesson for life

At age 30, Robert Moses learned that dreams without power to implement them are meaningless. For the rest of his life, Moses acquired power. In fact, Moses became so influential that during more than three decades, none of the state's six governors or the city's six mayors challenged him. He became the country's greatest builder, pushing through billions of dollars of public works projects, including highways, beaches, power dams, campgrounds, parks, play-grounds, and hundreds of miles of expressways.

By his life's end, Moses had changed. He loved power for power's sake and lost the idealistic dreams he once had for good government. But his lessons stand today for every good-hearted person with a passion to better the world, particularly through government and its vast bureaucracies.

Three lessons

What are those lessons? There are many, but I will cite only three.

First, good ideas must be borne from a spiritual base. Robert Moses relinquished his passion for good government and apparently lost his soul in the drive to amass power. For many, this spiritual base is Jesus' desire for justice and mercy, justice for the poor, compassion for the suffering, and hope for the helpless. Faith in God, and the strength and perseverance this gives us, can carry us through difficult times in the pursuit of these goals.

Second—and this is important for the idealistic among us—good ideas alone are useless. Without what Robert Moses called "executive support," ideas will not become reality. That's where politics—politics in a generic sense—enters in, yes, even in the world of education.

Third, the "dark" world of politics provides tools of enormous influence. Politically powerful people can accomplish Christ's mandate in a big way. For example, outside my Chicago office, I often encounter the homeless and may give them a dollar. But in one afternoon, an administrator I know conceived of a $4 million program for the homeless. He provided jobs to landscape median strips in the city.

Another leader I know worked successfully for the Community Reinvestment Act, which poured billions of dollars into poor communities in home loan programs. Both used their political savvy to accomplish good.

In Chicago Public Schools, the management team appointed in 1995 by Mayor Richard M. Daley has posted enormous successes. Although there is still a long way to go, test scores, enrollments, and attendance have risen across the board.

For example:

- One program—now a nationwide model—ends the practice of promoting children to the next grade simply because they have aged a year. It provides intense reading and math lessons in mandatory summer school for those lagging behind their peers.

- The school system won enough credibility with the bond-rating services to launch a $2.5 billion capital improvement program to replace and repair aging schools. Buildings across the city have a new face.

- America's third largest school system, known for labor strife year after year, marked four years of peace with its teachers' union and recently signed another four-year labor agreement.

- A zero-tolerance policy for drugs and weapons in schools resulted in hundreds of children being expelled and then sent to special schools for disruptive children, greatly enhancing school safety.

- Corruption has been targeted through offices such as my own, which investigates waste, fraud, and abuse. A system not known for firing anyone increased the number of dismissals.

- The management team introduced common sense measures such as allowing principals to hire business managers, instituting stricter standards for principals, and enrolling students in the spring. Previously, students enrolled in the fall and, as a result, hundreds of students went without teachers as late as October because of the time required to assign teachers based on enrollment.

There are other examples. A truancy hotline. After-school programs. A unit to help principals navigate the maze of rules to remediate or dismiss poorly performing teachers. The list goes on.

All this and far more was accomplished in the backdrop of an intensely political atmosphere within the system. Many of us good-hearted people have shunned internal politics because it means doing things for something other than the right reason. It means building alliances with people for whom we have little respect, knowing when not to speak out and, on occasion, softening a hard line on political ideology. It means being harsh at times. Some view this as contradictory to biblical teaching on humility, gentleness, and kindness.

But spiritual leaders in the Bible could be very tough. Take King David, for example. When he picked his management team, he selected mighty warriors known for such accomplishments as single-handedly killing 800 men in one encounter.

Many wonder how the Old Testament prophets could be so violent in their pronouncements. It is a mystery until one asks the question, "What did the people do that was so offensive to God?" The answer? Among other things, *they burned their children alive, as a religious ritual.*

Certainly, pouring tens of thousands of dropouts onto the streets and graduating untold numbers of children with ACT scores of 17 because we failed to teach them is also offensive to God. It robs these children of a future. Such practices require a strong response.

Good people who shun politics allow those with evil intentions to make major decisions affecting hundred of thousands of children. But when good people choose to become politically powerful, what they accomplish through God's providence and protection is immeasurable.

Succeeding in the bureaucracy of schools

To be successful in a school bureaucracy, we need to master the politics of the place. The question is how.

First, we should hire competent people with children's interests in mind. We save ourselves untold pain if we hire well. Our management ranks should be filled with brilliant, caring people. How do we avoid hiring mistakes? There are Web sites and books that provide guidance on the subject. *Hiring the Best* is one such book. When I hire, I ask for six references and samples of a candidate's work product. I give an onsite test to determine how the candidate thinks. Resumés (unless they are poorly done) and interviews are given last priority.

Second, we should mentor each other, promote each other, and protect each other. Corrupt people have done this for years in bureaucracies, thereby creating strangleholds on entire systems. They hire people with their own moral lapses so what they do does not seem so offensive. Or they hire incompetent staff. Such people do not object to wrongdoing or to poor decisions because they are unable to get jobs in private industry at the salaries they receive. Some shortsighted administrators hire weak people because they do not pose a threat to them. Hiring is one task that should not be delegated to staff members, if at all possible. The most important function a manager can do well is hire well.

Third, we should delegate on other matters. By trusting, mentoring, training, and investing in our staffs, we spread our influence. In the book *Jesus CEO,* the author notes that Jesus delegated to his twelve disciples, and eleven of them carried on his legacy around the world long after he was gone.

Fourth, we must be willing to fire staff when necessary. Most of you will never face internal sabotage but, in large, ineffective bureaucracies, sabotage is an art form. Dangerous people, who know instinctively what to say to gain a manager's trust, can take down entire operations by their actions. Often they exercise control by their knowledge of systems and rules involving crucial operations such as payroll, purchasing, or the filling of positions. Institutional knowledge is important, but we must understand human nature. Anyone who loses power, apart from the grace of God, is a potential saboteur. Think about it. What incentive does such a person have to see your new regime succeed?

One new superintendent of a statewide agency flattened his organization, combining departments and demoting department heads. But he kept them on. They became his worst enemies, sniping at him during his entire term and leaking negative information to the media. In the end, their missteps—which he refused to correct by swift dismissal—resulted in his removal. The book *The 48 Laws of Power*, although distasteful, clearly explains the mindset.

Fifth, we should network and maintain a cadre of supporters. We should build a circle of good-hearted people to whom we can turn for encouragement and support. For me, this includes an array of Christians with unshakable faith in God's protection. This strategy keeps us strong when work gets rocky. It also creates a network of favors, but favors that benefit children. Such favors may, for example, consist of helping a suicidal child into a hospital or financing a beneficial program. Or it may be advocating for a department head whose reputation has been unjustly smeared because that person is an agent of change.

Further, those of us who wish to make a difference must understand how evil thinks. Large bureaucracies provide billions of dollars in contracts, job security, enormous power, and often high wages. Many are attracted to them by less than honorable motives.

These same bureaucracies often spit out good people and squash them like bugs on the sidewalk. Such people may have learned Jesus' mandate to be as innocent as doves, but they ignored the first half of the missive: to be shrewd as serpents. Armed with good intentions, they end up bitter, sometimes unaware of the sabotage that undermined them.

The shepherds, the wolves, and the lambs

To survive, we need to overcome naiveté. The best way I can explain this is through an analogy of wolves and lambs. Wolves are persons who take no responsibility for their actions. They live to destroy, and blame the lambs for the things of which they are guilty. In a work situation, they lodge accusations in areas where they are guilty to confuse the picture for superiors or even the public. Wolves may portray themselves as victims and use flattery to achieve their goals. They believe themselves to be smarter than the lambs because they are willing to do things lambs would never consider. They scheme and portray truth as lies and lies as truth.

The lambs, on the other hand, take the guilt of the wolves on their shoulders. Good-hearted, they treat the wolf with respect and kindness, not understanding the wolf's nature or intentions. Lambs are often victims.

The goal is to be a shepherd, who protects the lambs and fights the wolves. The shepherd is wary enough to see evil coming and to shelter the flock. Part of being a shepherd in a highly political, historically ineffective and difficult organization is understanding the tools that are used against us to make us ineffective.

The weapons others use

One such tool is distractions. We may be taken off focus in any number of ways. We may be loaded with meaningless work or requests. We may be engaged in firefights, battles over issues that have nothing to do with children. We may even face harassment and threats, all designed to upset us and to keep us off balance for days. The solution is to ignore such nonsense and remain calm and focused. That really irritates enemies who otherwise take joy in frantic reactions.

Second, enemies may target very real weaknesses in a department. Our departments or agencies must be run well, free of bookkeeping errors, sloppiness in adhering to state laws, and without significant violations of rules. Carelessness in areas such as expenses, for example, can ruin a career. The best protection against such attacks is a strong product. It is difficult to target a superintendent who has posted increased test scores or, in my case, a person who heads a department that has produced accurate, thorough, and significant investigations. Of course, having a good product works only if people know about it. Marketing that product with the school board, the mayor, or, if appropriate, the public, protects us and our teams.

A third weapon that may be used against us is an unfathomable maze of rules and regulations. This creates a system of gatekeepers. They decide who passes—that is, who is granted waivers of the rules—and who doesn't. Those who are irritating do not pass. New leaders of ailing bureaucracies should immediately target areas such as purchasing, human resources, budgeting, and computer systems. It is crucial to bring in loyal managers to control such functions, which, if ineffective, can grind the entire system to a halt. Having loyal team members who understand the issues and have the authority to retool those systems is critical.

A fourth way through which leaders are made ineffective is inaccurate information. When our management team arrived in 1995, Gery Chico, President of the Chicago Board of Education, and Chief Executive Officer Paul Vallas did something no previous leadership team had done. They bypassed bureaucracy and went straight to the schools to cull ideas on improving the system. Often their own management teams had provided inaccurate information, either because they had not visited the front lines or were not willing to admit their mistakes. One helpful tip is to request all audits for the last five years and read them carefully.

Also understand that, in going into difficult situations, unhelpful staff may attempt to manipulate through jargon and the knowledge of those systems. I do not accept explanations I do not understand. I typically tell those who attempt to throw up smoke screens, "I am not a stupid woman. Please explain in English." Only through specific, detailed questions do I learn the root of the problem and its common sense cure. And, of course, I go to multiple sources for information, building a network of middle managers and the "little people" who provide important information.

A fifth method is intimidation. Street fighters know this tactic well. Good-hearted people often run the opposite direction when confronted with hardball tactics. For some battles, battles over egos for example, running may be an appropriate way to preserve energy. But other battles are worth fighting. They include battles over tools to do the job. In the beginning of my tenure, I willingly relinquished some valuable tools in an effort to get along with people. The decision nearly crippled my operations. When someone attacks my tools or attempts to throw up an array of unwritten rules to stop my progress, I demand to see the rule in writing, or ascertain whether or not it indeed is a "Maribeth rule"—a rule created for me and no one else. I have yet to lose such a battle.

Intimidated no more

I do not get intimidated easily, nor do the other shepherds I know. I use whatever power I have to accomplish my goals. Often people who do not have children as their focus have committed some form of wrongdoing. To them, I am a terrible threat.

I once ran into a department head on a bus and asked her how she was doing. She replied, "Guess what? I don't cry anymore." A vibrant Christian, she used to cry about harassing phone calls, charges that she was incompetent and of the wrong race, and constant challenges to her mandates that employees arrive on time. The employees had not been supervised or required to report on their work product for more than a decade. She changed that. Today, she is building important programs for children across the city. Like me, this once good-hearted lamb, who was nearly defeated, rose up in strength as a shepherd and learned to use power to challenge those without the children's interests at heart.

Both of us learned that power respects power. Power for its own sake does not respect goodness, kindness, integrity, or competence. To be successful, we may need to appeal to the offending person's self-interests or fears. For example, one science teacher begged her principal for new textbooks for three years. The principal consistently maintained that money to replace the obsolete books was unavailable. In the fourth year, science scores dropped. The principal ordered new textbooks the same day. Had the teacher figured out earlier what the principal cared most about—her image—the teacher might have been far more successful in arguing her case.

For those of us who are called to leadership roles, we should acquire the legitimate and appropriate power for that position and use it wisely and as necessary to protect the lambs and to fulfill the mission of quality education for all the children entrusted to us.

Without that power, ideas on how to change government, bureaucracies, or school systems are only that—just ideas. But as we wisely and carefully use that power, we can find fulfillment and the rewards that come to us as we participate in the consummation of our important and challenging mission—the education of children.

Maribeth VanderWeele

Chapter 6

Dealing with the News Media

In 1988, then United States Secretary of Education William Bennett called Chicago schools the "worst in America." Today, both Bennett and the White House praise Chicago school reform as a nationwide model.

What made the difference? A team appointed by Mayor Richard M. Daley that worked long hours in a whirlwind effort to implement common sense reforms that led to consistently higher student achievement.

Chicago's school reform

Chances are most of you have heard at least part of this story. After all, Chicago's reforms have received nationwide acclaim and are being modeled across the country. What you may not know is the intensive and brilliant marketing effort that brought these reforms to the nation's eye. It all began with exposing corruption in a scandal-plagued system.

For the first time, exposés were generated not by the newspapers or the federal government but by our own administration. (When the mayor's reform effort began in 1995, I was part of the school management team.) While the previous regimes recounted for years that they had cut to the bone and that there was no more waste in the system, School Board President Gery Chico and Chief Executive Officer Paul Vallas unleashed example after example of waste and corruption.

On a 100-degree summer day—a slow news time, by the way—
we invited the television cameras to a warehouse filled with new
desks, chairs, and pianos that had been unused for years. Our team
sent the furniture and equipment to schools. On television, one local
school council member looked amazed as he recounted how the
school requested and immediately received furniture. "We didn't
even know anyone," he said.

Then there was the story of a million dollars in unnecessary
phone costs. The former managers leased rotary phones.

We unveiled a series of exposés on corrupt principals. One had
paid bribes to keep his job; another had lived in a school and constructed a shower in his office to accommodate his lifestyle. The list
goes on.

None of our predecessors had done this before. For years, the
bureaucracy had been on the defensive, denying the system was corrupt and inefficient, shrugging off as anomalies convictions of major
players in the system, including the former board president. When
we came in, Paul Vallas, the chief executive officer, and Gery Chico,
the new board president, became known as corruption fighters.

The media loved it. For one thing, Paul and Gery did the
reporters' jobs for them on slow news days. More importantly, I
think, many in the media genuinely wanted to see the system
improve. Our management team confirmed the media's worst suspicions. All of a sudden, it was as if the media and the management
were partners against the bad guys. I keep expecting the press hon-
eymoon to end, but four years later, with few exceptions, it still has
not, perhaps because of the deep ties developed in that first year.

Building credibility

The media effort brought much needed credibility to the system's management. Gery Chico has a saying: In government, never
promise what you cannot deliver, deliver what you promise, and
market what you have delivered. This brings credibility, support, and
money to your efforts. He and Paul Vallas understood that the system needed credibility with the parents to persuade them to send

their children to Chicago's schools. It needed credibility with the legislature to ensure sympathetic laws. It needed credibility with the
bond holders to launch what has become a $2.5 billion capital pro-
gram. Such a program was unheard of in a system that had not been
able to borrow funds since a financial collapse two decades ago.

For many of you, marketing your school district by discussing
corruption is untenable. It is true that your circumstances may be
different than that of the nation's third largest school system, but the
central lesson is universal: Being up-front with problems and map-
ping out solutions builds credibility with the media. Pretending
problems do not exist creates adversarial relationships.

When the press calls

This is among many tips I learned not only as a reporter for two
decades but now as an administrator. To begin with, when the press
descends on you en masse over an unfolding story, quickly pull
together your talking points and have a staff member take notes of
any questions for which information is not immediately available.
Ensure that all key administrators involved in the matter sign off on
the talking points to ensure their accuracy—and do it quickly.

The operative word here is "speed." Deadlines are the lifeblood
of reporters. If you blow their deadlines, their stories will rely on the
facts or opinions of someone else. Their stories, without your view-
point in them, will be less accurate. That is your responsibility, not
theirs.

I still get phone calls from the media asking me to slip them
public information such as whether a certain person was employed
by the school system or whether we do business with a certain con-
tractor. I get them the information in ten to thirty minutes. Such
simple assistance builds rapport.

Related to the issue of speed is accessibility. Paul Vallas has given
both his home and pager numbers to every member of the media he
meets. He pays a high price in terms of privacy, but his school system is hailed as a nationwide model as a result.

I once asked a radio reporter why she quoted a certain activist who had no accomplishments to her name and little credibility. The answer was blunt: The activist is accessible. Reporters need quotes. And they need stories. Paul feeds reporters a constant spate of news.

As chief executive officer, Paul Vallas is extremely successful with the press for another reason. He speaks in layman's language. Use of educational jargon raises suspicions. Reporters—trained in the art of clarity—view jargon as a smokescreen to obscure what a public official really thinks.

What harm results when you express outrage that a bus driver carelessly left a child on a bus or, in worst-case scenarios, a teacher is alleged to have molested a child? Express your grief about a shooting. Build connections to the audience and disassociate yourself from the troublemaker. Just make sure that, if anyone is implicated, your facts are correct. If only an arrest has occurred, speak in caveats. For example:

"If the allegations prove to be true, we are outraged and hurt at this betrayal of trust. But we must be careful; no allegations have been verified."

Another rule of thumb: Be honest. If you cannot talk about something, say so. If the media call about something gone awry, prepare an immediate action plan. Admit mistakes and explain what measures are being taken to avoid them in the future.

The best way to dodge bad press, of course, is to avoid mistakes in the first place and to sensitize staff members about what can blow up in the media. The New York City school system was mired for a year in controversy over a few lines in a curriculum depicting gay families. The irony was that few teachers read the curriculum.

In another state, a superintendent was brought down partly by a publicly funded limousine ride. Because my staff is so sensitized to potential attacks, we actually debated about whether our water coolers would invite a press hit. I took the "courageous" stand that I was willing to defend their use. Admittedly, this is extreme, but I would rather they be overzealous on this issue than allow me to be blindsided.

Dealing with attacks from opponents

Agents of change can expect attacks from opponents, the source of most bad press. In dealing with such people, I believe in a three-step process:

First, attempt reconciliation. Many times, opponents simply want to be heard and respected.

If that does not work and attacks go public, counteract opposition with facts, not emotion. One principal friend of mine walked into the toughest high school in Chicago, mired not only with gang and staff problems but in fierce local politics. A community activist brought hundreds of parents to a school council meeting to claim they did not have input in major decisions. The principal calmly pulled out letter after letter inviting the activist, school council members, and parents to meetings that they declined to attend. She avoided personal attacks on the activist and focused on her plans to fill every classroom with textbooks, a radical idea at the time. Unflappable, the principal turned the parents into her biggest supporters.

Finally, if all else fails, go on the offensive. Once again, Paul Vallas is a master at this. Education reform groups that previously were seen as experts on Chicago education have been marginalized in their criticism. Vallas frankly pointed out to the media, time and time again, that the reforms of these groups have been unsuccessful and they have few, if any, accomplishments. His pronouncements are accompanied by appropriate indignation.

If, despite these efforts, the media quote misinformed critics, the best step is to correct errors of fact through letters to the editors, particularly errors that involve you personally. Make the letters short, factual, and professional. Otherwise the errors will be repeated in the future. Researchers rely on newspaper articles to write history. Reporters rely on old clips to produce overview articles. Future employers check newspaper articles to make hiring decisions. Your decision to let errors of fact stand unchallenged may affect your career years down the road. I have seen people blackballed because of a negative and incorrect article from years ago that they never challenged. Regardless of the truth, employers do not want to admit to the media that they just hired a new manager who had accusations of problems in the past. As managers, you yourselves probably shy away from such job candidates no matter how firmly they attribute such accusations to political opposition.

The best protection against attacks is having a strong product. If the press and the public know your agency or school system as successful, both are less likely to take attacks seriously. This requires communicating your successes.

Spreading the good news

But how, you may ask, does one get good news in the media? The best way is to first understand the needs of the media. The media's purpose is not to give you good publicity. It exists to inform, to enlighten, and to entertain a broad audience. Think about it. Would you read a story on scholarship winners if they had no connection to you, your family, or your school? Chances are you would not.

Your challenge is to develop an interesting story that incidentally gives your school system good press. Think about your college fiction course. What interests readers? Stories of conflict, of human interest, of people overcoming odds, or doing something unusual or unprecedented.

A friend asked me to critique her press release about the groundbreaking of a school addition. The release began with the date, time, and purpose of the event. Included in her materials, but not in the press release, were fascinating stories of Bosnian immigrants who overcame life-threatening circumstances to get to America and consequently to the school. I advised her to begin her press release with three such stories, each summarized within a few sentences. The fourth paragraph should explain how these families would converge at the groundbreaking of the school addition. This is typical newspaper format. Anecdotes are crucial. So are home phone numbers of those you suggest to be interviewed.

The press release should also provide a context and comparisons. If you can say "unprecedented," do so. It helps the reporter determine the importance. The best time to float story ideas is prior to holidays, when many reporters are on vacation. They need to stockpile and, once again, ideas with facts spelled out and sources available on weekends get priority. Bad news stories can be floated during a national crisis or at 4 p.m. on Fridays.

Speaking of national crises, if your students are working on a project connected to a national news event, contact the media that same day. Newspapers in particular are looking for what are called "sidebars" in those circumstances.

Finally, think visually. Originally, our warehouse story was to be told from a podium in the central office. I convinced the team to bring it to the warehouse on a 100-degree day. The result was national exposure to our corruption-fighting efforts.

Four years later, people still talk about that image of the stockpiled furniture while children sat on milk crates. Had the story been explained from a podium, it never would have had the impact.

Dr. Beverly L. Hall
Superintendent
Atlanta Public Schools

During her distinguished career, Beverly Hall has served as a school principal, superintendent of a community school district, and Deputy Chancellor for Instruction for New York City Public Schools. In 1995, she was appointed State District Superintendent of Newark Public Schools, the largest school district in New Jersey. In March 1999, she was appointed Superintendent of Atlanta Public Schools.

Dr. Hall's accomplishments have been recognized in both the public and private sectors. She received her B.A. and M.S. degrees from Brooklyn College, and her doctorate from Fordham University.

Beverly L. Hall

Chapter 7

Lessons Learned— Newark Four Years Later

The New Jersey State Department of Education monitors its schools by a process which is, according to state documents, "designed to ensure that all districts have in place the elements of a thorough and efficient educational system and are meeting state standards." In 1995 the state, having conducted an intensive investigation of the Newark School District, found just cause to take over the system and replace the Board of Education with a state-operated school district.

After a careful review of practices in the school district, deficiencies were found to exist in virtually every aspect of the management of the Newark Public Schools. Citations were issued in the areas of educational programs, governance, finance, and management. New Jersey's largest school district, with 43,000 students, had experienced a trickle-down effect as a result of gross mismanagement. And over the years, corruption and dysfunction at the uppermost levels of the system manifested themselves in teachers' lowered expectations of students, which resulted in poor performance by the students—the standard by which the public most readily measures the success of its schools.

Setting the stage for real reform

However unpleasant the process was at times and continues to be, the state's takeover of the district has facilitated a process of reform unencumbered by the typical obstacles of patronage and the politics of status quo so prevalent in Newark. By removing some of those elements which had become impediments to providing the children of Newark a thorough and efficient education, the state tried to wipe the slate clean in order that necessary changes could be instituted swiftly. I was appointed Superintendent by the State Commissioner of Education and given five years to turn Newark around. The clock began ticking July 1, 1995.

The state intervention legislation permitted us to introduce important changes in the culture of the district, to focus on student achievement above all else, and to lay the foundation for future growth in the Newark Public Schools.

By the end of the first year, we had reorganized the district in order to redirect $26.3 million into educational programs for students. These included full-day kindergarten, staff developers in math and reading, new textbooks, and guidance counselors in every elementary school. We also cleaned up the horrific and unhealthy physical conditions of buildings, hired more security guards, and created an internal investigative unit to uncover the corrupt and/or unethical practices that had long plagued Newark schools.

This realignment of priorities and budget involved the difficult task of laying off some 600 employees in July 1996. The layoffs were traumatic, a shock to a system that had taken easy employment for granted. The situation was an easy issue for the vested interest groups to exploit and misrepresent to the community. Without those layoffs, our reform agenda might have been easier to introduce or more readily embraced. However, without the shifting of dollars, we would not have been able to put needed resources into the classroom.

There were other things we were able to do as a state-operated district that could not have been done previously in the Newark schools. The takeover legislation permitted us to dismiss any tenured building principal or vice-principal for inefficiency, incapacity, unbecoming conduct, or other documented causes. By the end of my tenure, as a result of a rigorous assessment process, 50 percent of the principals were new to their position. Many of those who were replaced had attained their position as part of the patronage system that had long existed in Newark, and were incapable of providing the leadership necessary to create an environment where students can achieve and excel.

Implementing the reform plan

Beyond those drastic measures taken during the first year, we began implementation of an ambitious five-year strategic plan that focused on improving student performance. In March of 1999, our fourth year of state operation, I was able to report that we were beginning to see a rise in student test performance.

Of course, test scores alone do not tell the full story. From 1995 to 1999, we introduced a number of important changes to improve the environment for teaching and learning in the Newark Public Schools, through our strategic plan. These programs and innovations put children first and form the rock-solid foundation upon which the district will build in the years ahead.

Several programs and initiatives bear singling out for what I believe will be their long-term impact. Certainly, universal full-day kindergarten ranks among the most important programs that we made available to the children of Newark. Similarly, the emphasis on meaningful staff development, which we initiated the first year and have continued to emphasize, has long-term significance for the way teaching and learning evolve in the district.

Other initiatives that bear highlighting include:

- The introduction of Project GRAD which, by way of staff development and the incentive of scholarships, aims to increase student performance, increase graduation rates, and increase the number of students who go on to college.

- The development of a new promotion policy to end social promotion and provide meaningful intervention for students before they are held back, and to ensure that new methods of teaching are employed if students are held back.

- Community partnerships which helped us to extend the hours schools are open, including high quality after-school programs at schools throughout the city.

- An attendance improvement strategy that resulted in a 30-year high for student attendance.

- A new comprehensive discipline policy so that students clearly understand their rights and responsibilities in the class-room.

- The introduction of standards for allocating staff and supplies. When we first arrived, principals had no idea how resources for their schools were determined and had no input into the budget process for their schools.

- The placement of custodial staff under the direct control of principals to provide for greater accountability at the school level.

Also among our most successful initiatives are those that have engaged parents and the wider community in the improvement of our public schools. Those include:

- School-based health clinics that have brought basic services to some of our most needy children and eventually will provide services to the families of those children as well.

- Parent volunteer academies, which bring parents into the schools to help, have significantly improved parent-school relationships.

- The Parent Leadership Development Institute, which focuses on developing the next generation of parent leaders.

- School Management Teams to facilitate decentralization of the district by engaging parents, administrators, teachers, and the community in school-based decision-making.

What the legislation missed

The state takeover legislation permitted us to aggressively institute our strategic plan. But it was silent on an issue that is crucial to raising the level of student performance: the expeditious removal of non-performing teaching staff.

The most significant obstacles standing in the way of reform in this area are tenure laws, civil service regulations, and labor agreements that we inherited. These statutes, rules, and contracts that are intended to protect employee rights often hamper our ability to take action against undesirable employees.

Tenure laws. New Jersey's tenure laws restrict the district's ability to discipline or remove tenured teachers. Even under state intervention, the tenure law prohibits school districts from reducing a teacher's pay, much less terminating a teacher's employment, unless tenure charges are filed. This process typically lasts two years, involves a number of agencies, and can cost the district as much as $120,000 to take a case to its final phase.

Civil service regulations. Newark Public Schools is also one of only nine school districts in the state that are governed by civil service statutes and rules. These statutes and rules have created an inefficient hiring system and disciplinary process that protect employee rights to the detriment of students. Most non-instructional employees in the Newark Public Schools, approximately 2,700 individuals, fall into this category. Employees in career service positions, similar to tenured teachers, can only be removed for cause. The progressive disciplinary process can take a year or longer and again may involve a number of agencies and courts. Final decisions can be overturned by a state panel, which means, ultimately, the district still may not be able to remove an employee. Eligibility to work in a non-instructional post in the Newark schools is determined by geographic preferences, veteran status, and position-specific test results, all of which dictate whom a district must hire to fill vacancies. Management's preference for a hardworking employee deserving of a promotion is meaningless if the employee is not within the top three on a list of candidates deemed eligible by civil service priorities.

Labor agreements. Labor agreements also define the terms and conditions of employment in the Newark Public Schools. The district has inherited provisions from these agreements that are both costly and tremendously inefficient.

One such provision which we successfully eliminated was terminal leave, which allowed a teacher or principal to retire in January, the middle of the school year, and draw their full salary until June—leaving students to pick up as best as they can with a substitute teacher or new building leader. Terminal leave is a good name for it, given the effect it has on sound classroom practices and continuity. This provision had a fatal effect on the morale of students and staff who were left behind and dire consequences for the quality of teaching and learning—not to mention the expense associated with paying a full-time substitute while also paying the salary and benefits of a tenured teacher or principal.

We also redefined funeral leave, which in the past had been so rampantly abused that some employees claimed the death of a close friend on a regular basis in order to get a paid day off. We also scaled back the number of paid holidays for 12-month employees from 19 to 17 days per year. By way of comparison, a typical number of paid holidays in the private sector averages 12 days per year. These were small but significant victories in winning back time for students. (In fact, we were also able to introduce a slightly longer school day.) Despite these improvements, we were still bound by other contractual provisions. For example:

- A prohibition against establishing and assigning employees to new work-shift schedules.

- Wage rates for certain non-instructional employee groups that are double the prevailing rates for the Newark area.

- Overtime rates for building principals and other management groups.

- Benefit packages that far exceed comparable public and private sector offerings.

Where provisions of collective bargaining agreements seem to be in violation of state law, requests have been filed with the New Jersey Public Employment Relations Commission (PERC) to examine those provisions outside the scope of bargaining.

Circumventing some obstacles

Despite these obstacles, however, there are signs of progress:

- Principals are getting the message that they will be supported by management in their decisions to take disciplinary action against non-performing teachers. For example, the first significant action that can be taken using the progressive discipline approach is the withholding of pay increments. Prior to state intervention, pay increments were withheld only 61 times in 30 years across the system. In 1998 alone, there were 67 such increments withheld.

- New standards have been developed this year to aid principals in the evaluation of non-tenured teachers, and new protocols for attaining tenure are being developed.

- A state-of-the-art human resources/payroll system has been installed to better monitor employee attendance and to eliminate abuse of leave time.

Governance, leadership, and return to local control

In addition to teacher quality, there are other issues crucial to Newark school reform that the state legislation never addressed and which merit examination. These include the issues of governance, leadership, and return to local control.

There was no clear rationale for having fifteen members on the Advisory Board, which replaced the nine-member school board. The law called for the Commissioner of Education to appoint thirteen Advisory Board members, and the City Council of Newark to appoint two. What was clear from our board meetings, especially in those first two years, was that the legislation should have prohibited former board members from serving on the Advisory Board. The board members appointed by the City Council were the most disruptive members and prevented others from functioning those first two years.

The legislation also called for board elections to begin this past spring, with the fifteen members running for nine seats. Advisory Board members felt they had just begun to work well together as a team these last two years and so requested a postponement of elections until next year. The result was that New Jersey's Commissioner of Education appointed nine members from among the fifteen. The first open elections of three board members will be in the spring of 2000.

However, we should also consider whether the election of nine people is the true watermark of return to local control. We must be specific about what local control is and is not. In fact, instead of a "return" to anything, it would be more accurate to speak of a revival of democracy and community involvement in the school district. What existed in the district prior to state operation was anything but democratic, and control lay in a few powerful hands. Only a fraction of the eligible voters in Newark even bothered to vote in school board elections.

We must also be frank about the community ambivalence around our school reform agenda. State operation created a great deal of animosity and forced many people to take sides. There was little preparation among the grassroots community, especially among those who were fed up with the old way of doing things. The layoff of some 600 employees, mainly transportation and food service workers, certainly clouded the issue. Those superfluous jobs cost the district money and diverted funds from the classroom, but that was a hard point to make in a community starved for jobs and job security. Although the district set up job counseling and a referral system, there was no jobs program or political proposal offered to take the sting out of that reorganization. Generations of Newark families had come to depend on the district for employment. Once again, the schools were expected to do it all, and the students, ultimately, bore the consequences.

Another factor that undermined or muted support for our reforms was the lack of closure with the past. There is a real connection between corruption and low-performing school systems. But the legislation is tentative where it should be definitive about why state operation is necessary. There was no swift followup through the criminal justice system to demonstrate that there had indeed been great wrongdoing in the Newark Public Schools, and that it had exacted a harsh price in the classroom.

There were no indictments of those who had carried out the criminal policies described by the state in its Comprehensive Compliance Investigation, or CCI report. The CCI was a catalog of the abuses and misuses of power in the district and formed the basis of the takeover. But there was a great silence on who was responsible and who would be held accountable. Absent an aggressive strategy to follow through with criminal indictments, the CCI was reduced to just another partisan document. In the void, you could hear the voices from the old regime saying confidently, "We'll wait you out. This too shall pass."

Drastic measures in drastic situations

Despite these flaws in the legislation and despite the controversy engendered, I remain convinced that state operation of the Newark Public Schools was absolutely necessary to take control of the schools from leaders who were abusing their power, and to lay a foundation for lasting reform. More states are examining the governance structures in their troubled school districts. The Education Commission of the States notes that twenty-two states have academic bankruptcy laws that allow states to "take over" local district operations in cases of poor student performance. Among these are

Alabama, Arkansas, Connecticut, Iowa, Massachusetts, Missouri, New Mexico, Pennsylvania, South Carolina, and, yes, even Georgia.

Another variation on this theme is the "mayoral takeover." Chicago, Boston, Cleveland, Baltimore, and now Detroit have all seen their governors and city leaders step up to the plate. In 1995, The Illinois State Legislature shifted control of the Chicago Public Schools to Mayor Richard M. Daley and charged him with appointing school board members. The Inspector General of the Chicago Public Schools, Maribeth VanderWeele, has already shared some information on that situation. In Massachusetts, the state Legislature abolished the elected Boston School Committee and gave the mayor of Boston the right to appoint school committee members. In 1996, the citizens of Boston voted to maintain the mayoral-appointed school committee. Mayor Thomas M. Menino of Boston recently addressed a group of education writers and said, "The single day I'm most proud of as mayor is the day I assumed responsibility for what happens in the Boston Public Schools. By making myself accountable, I have led the way for others to make themselves accountable, too." Boston Superintendent Thomas Payzant is one of the longest serving urban superintendents as a result, I believe, of this working partnership with the mayor.

Both Chicago's mayor and Boston's mayor recognize that the revitalization of their cities is inextricably entwined with the success of their public schools. While the jury is still out on the effectiveness of mayoral control of school districts on long-term student achievement, both mayors have stepped up to the plate in admirable fashion. And unlike Newark's mayor, neither has spoken in an incendiary fashion. Instead, they have placed education at the top of the urban agenda and formed alliances across the political spectrum.

I worry that the displaced vested interest groups will convince others that in New Jersey the takeover has failed and that there will be a rush to return districts to local control. I encourage everyone to look at the national trend and stand firm. Newark is not ready and, in my mind, should not be returned until an appropriate governance structure that will provide protection for the children is put in place.

Absent the kind of mayoral leadership that has enabled Chicago, Boston, and now Detroit to build formidable coalitions for change, the state of New Jersey would have failed the children of Newark had it simply remained a bystander to the spiraling decline of the system. But reviving our urban schools will not yield immediate gratification. It is a long-range investment.

Continuing Newark's reform process

During my four years in Newark, we were able to bring much-needed stability to the district, halting the downward spiral. I believe the toughest challenge for this next chapter in Newark's history will be to address the issues of unionism and governance, which are impossible to take on without support in all the right places. But they must be addressed if real long-term change is to occur, and if the children of Newark are to have the quality school system that they truly deserve.

Is there any hope for this system which has been plagued for so long by mediocrity at best, negligence at worst? Absolutely. But it will not be turned around overnight, and it will require leadership that has the ability to focus on the students and resists the interference of state and local politics, which have nothing whatsoever to do with the best interests of children and everything to do with the interests of adults.

Dr. David G. Myers
John Dirk Werkman
Professor of Psychology
Hope College

David G. Myers is a social psychologist whose work as researcher, teacher, and author has been widely acclaimed. His introductory psychology textbook is the most widely studied psychology text, and his scientific research has appeared in various journals.

Dr. Myers has digested psychological research for the lay public through twelve books and in articles in magazines ranging from *Scientific American* to *Christian Century.*

A graduate of Whitworth College, Dr. Myers received his Ph.D. from the University of Iowa.

David G. Myers

Chapter 8

The American Paradox

I'm sure that in your community, as in the culture at large, there has been a lot of conversation about what is going on in American culture, how this is impacting American youth, and what this means for you as school administrators. Though I can't give specific answers to the latter question, I would like to give you an overall glimpse, a bird's-eye view if you will, of trends in American culture since 1960. As we come to the end of this century and the end of the millennium, this seems like a good time to take stock of what has been happening, and develop fresh vision and focus for ourselves and our schools for the century we're about to begin.

In this lecture we'll be looking at some contrasting sets of values. On the one hand, individualism and materialism have become dominant. Surveys indicate that college students are giving increasing priority to material values; the number who say that it's very important or essential that they become "very well off financially" has nearly doubled—from 40 to 74 percent. However, these values can be contrasted with an alternative value system that gives emphasis to our human connections, particularly the bonds we have with one another in families and in communities, including communities of faith. I see a reemergence of cultural priority being given to close relationships and spirituality and a receding of individualism and materialism, which have been in ascendancy over the last forty years.

A great time to be alive

Before I elaborate on these trends, I want to celebrate with you and have you think about why, despite events that may plague your school system, these are really great times to be alive. Would you really rather be living 50 or 100 years ago, at the time of your grandparents or great-grandparents? Or would you rather be alive today? Consider what life was like a century ago. Families were as often broken as they are today, but by premature death, when life expectancy was so much shorter than it is today. There was no social safety net as we have today. There were no child labor laws in America. Half the children were not in school because so many were working, whereas today we have universal and compulsory education. Women and minorities had restricted opportunities, compared to the advancement of human rights today and what this has made possible. People had so much less of the technology that we enjoy, such as the computers and technology that enhance education and enrich our lives today. We celebrate it—it's terrific. I love it!

However, despite these material advances, we have had some remarkable statements from national leaders. "Something is terribly awry with modern life." "Our decaying society needs a social values revolution." "We really have to have a fundamental sea change in values." Now, who do you think said those things? Was it Dan Quayle? James Dobson? George W. Bush? William Bennett? No. Actually those three statements were made respectively by Hillary Rodham Clinton, Jesse Jackson, and Marion Wright Edelman of the Children's Defense Fund.

I cite these examples to indicate that what I'm talking about today are not culture war issues. There are culture war issues; they have to do with abortion, gay rights, economics, and tax policies. We're not talking about those. We're talking about areas where the "new" Democrats and the "compassionate" Republicans are saying essentially the same thing for the very same reasons.

One could approach these issues through a series of powerful anecdotes that focus on the stories of people. However, my own predilection as a social scientist is instead to provide data that reveal the general truth.

My comments will focus on the period from 1960 to 1995, a period of significant advancement of human rights, and material and technological developments. These have been the best of times. But in this same period we have also witnessed a very significant and fascinating social recession, one that in its magnitude and its impact on human lives dwarfed the comparatively mild economic recessions that generated so much news during that time period. This social recession was defined by a doubling of the divorce rate, a tripling of the teen suicide rate, a quadrupling of the rate of reported violence as indexed by the FBI's annual uniform crime reports, a quintupling of the prison population, and a six-fold increase in the percentage of babies born to unmarried parents. I would note that beginning about 1994, many of these social indicators began to turn around in a more favorable direction.

In this lecture I will try to unpack some of these trends, and in doing so will be looking at many numbers. Bertrand Russell once said, "The mark of an educated person is the ability to look at a column of numbers and weep." Weep for the individuals, the real flesh and blood, the human lives that have been crushed and that are casualties of this social recession. This, it seems to me, when laid alongside the good news of material advance, defines The American Paradox, the title of my soon-to-be-published book.

This title, *The American Paradox,* refers to the fact that during the post-1960 years our income, in inflation-adjusted dollars, was skyrocketing upward along with many other good things that were happening in America, while simultaneously the civic health of the nation was going southward. The National Commission on Civic Renewal aggregated some two dozen indices of national civic health, including such factors as the health and well-being of children and of families and feelings of trust in one another. They aggregated those objective indices into an overall index of national civic health.

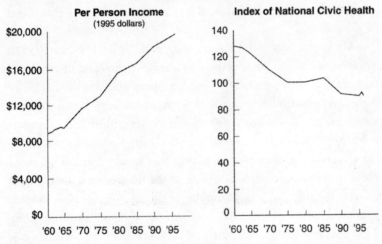

Figure 1.

Figure 1 shows both per person income and the Index of National Civic Health over the period 1960 to 1997.

Marriage and divorce

Let's examine some of the specific trends. As noted in Figure 2, the divorce rate has doubled since 1960. However, this increase in

Figure 2.

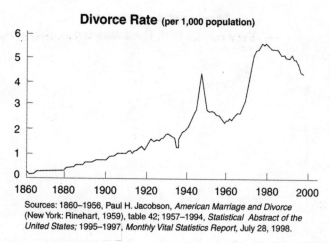

Figure 3.

divorce rate occurred mostly during the 1960s and 1970s, reaching its peak in the early 1980s, after which it actually leveled off and then tapered off a bit. This is partly due to the fact that people are marrying much later and marrying less often today than they did in the 1960–1980 era. People sometimes say that that's just a reflection of the abnormally high divorce rate that existed in the post-war years. However, if we take a longer review of history, we get a very different picture. From Figure 3, which shows the divorce rate for almost 140 years of American history, it is evident that the divorce rate has been going up ever since the mid-1800s, with a post-war blip in the 1940s. Apart from this, the divorce rate has increased steadily this whole century, until about 1985. I'm not saying, from my perspective, that marriage is a sacrament, or that divorce is always a bad thing. Sometimes a healthy new beginning is the optimal resolution for adults and children who are in very toxic or abusive situations. But nearly everyone, whether marrying for the first or second or third time, hopes that the relationship will be a satisfying, enduring, covenantal relationship for the rest of their lives. So anything we can do to make for healthy families and marriages is certainly not politically controversial.

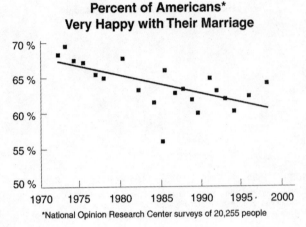

Percent of Americans*
Very Happy with Their Marriage

*National Opinion Research Center surveys of 20,255 people

Figure 4.

What do you think happened to marital happiness while the divorce rate increased? Today divorce is more socially acceptable. People divorce more often and are freer to leave an unhappy marriage. One might conclude, therefore, that married people are happier with their marriages today since they're freer to leave if they're unhappy. However, as is evident from the National Opinion Research Center surveys of Americans over the last twenty-five years (Figure 4), there has been a slight *decline* in the percent of Americans who report happiness in their marriages.

So there are two interesting trends. We are divorcing twice as often, and those who are still married are somewhat less happy with their marriages.

Moreover, we're marrying less often today in the United States. Today, 40 percent of adults are single, whereas back in 1960, 25 percent of adults were single. There is no longer a stigma associated with single adulthood today as there was in 1960, and we have singles programs in churches and singles bars and singles cruises. Our culture is more supportive of single adults.

Yet there is no question but that the state of marriage has been in very serious decline, and I don't know what other word could describe this trend. I would also note that we are talking about a very

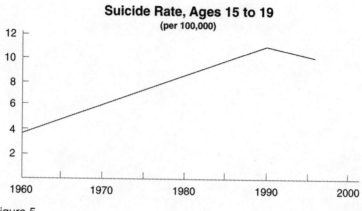

Figure 5.

thin slice of social history, a mere thirty-five-year period. That's an eye blink of time to any historian. So whatever else you think of these unprecedented phenomena, they certainly beg for a thoughtful understanding of what is really going on.

Suicide rate

Recently the Surgeon General declared suicide as a serious public health problem in the United States. Actually, adult suicide hasn't changed all that much over the last thirty-five years or so. But as Figure 5 indicates, there has been a dramatic increase in the teen suicide rate. There have also been increasing rates of depression in young adult Americans, including teens, college-aged students, younger adults, and the secondary school students with whom you deal. This no doubt relates to the near tripling of the teen suicide rate since 1960. It is gratifying that this rate has tapered off in recent years. Nevertheless, it's still 2½ times what it was back in 1960.

Violent crime

Public awareness of and concern about violent crime have greatly increased in recent years, particularly in view of a number of high-profile shootings that resulted in multiple deaths. Violent crime, as

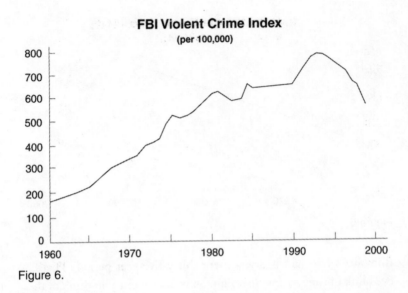

Figure 6.

indexed by the FBI, has increased dramatically since 1960, nearly four-fold, as indicated in Figure 6. The encouraging news is that violent crime during the last several years is on a significant decline.

Much of my focus in *The American Paradox* is on youth in America, and I have a special interest in violent crimes by juveniles. I spent considerable time trying to get accurate data on juvenile violent crime. Figure 7, the result of these efforts, shows the juvenile violent crime rate for 15- to 17-year-olds from 1960 to 1997. This rate shot up from 1960 to 1994, increasing more than four times. Since then a much-publicized drop in crime has occurred. We all celebrate this decline, although it still leaves us at about three times the juvenile violent crime rate of 1960. As we have noted, this is but one of many indicators that are now turning in a more positive direction.

Will these trends continue?

I started talking about these cultural trends in the early 1990s, when I became concerned about the trends we were seeing in these cultural parameters. My prediction at the end of each talk was always optimistic. I was confident that these trends would not continue at

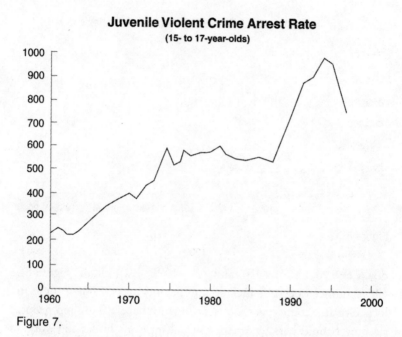

Juvenile Violent Crime Arrest Rate
(15- to 17-year-olds)

Figure 7.

this rate for another thirty-five years, because the toxicity of the trends would surely awaken public consciousness, setting in motion counterforces that would drive the pendulum in the other direction. For example, if the decline of family values is directly or indirectly related to the increase in juvenile violence, the culture will begin to awaken and be concerned, particularly when it is recognized that if these trends continue, there would be chaos after another thirty-five years.

Today's more favorable trends are complicated a bit by the very favorable economic circumstances and low unemployment. If we went into a serious economic recession, and unemployment increased, would we be confident that these favorable trends would continue?

Another factor is that because of increasing crime and use of drugs, we've had a significant increase in law enforcement and arrests and convictions. As a result, there has been a tremendous increase in our state and federal prison population, from 213,000 back in 1960,

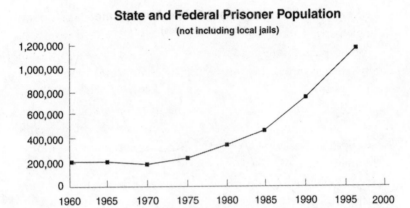

State and Federal Prisoner Population
(not including local jails)

Figure 8.

down to 196,000 in 1970, and as of 1997, 1.2 million (Figure 8). This number does not include another nearly 600,000 people in local city and county jails. So right now we have 1.8 million people sleeping behind bars in America, which gives us by far the world's highest rate of incarceration. This dramatic increase in incarceration and much more rigorous sentencing of those convicted partially explain the decline in the violent crime rate, because most of those who are in prison have committed multiple crimes and are now off the streets. I would add that this is done at great social cost. What we pay for prisons is approaching what we pay for schools.

Children born to unmarried parents

A matter of great concern to many people, and particularly to you as leaders in education, is the dramatic increase in the percent of babies born to unmarried parents in the United States. This trend is shown in Figure 9. From 1940 to 1960, the rate was less than 5 percent. But beginning about 1970 and continuing for more than two decades, something changed dramatically in the United States. As of 1997, 32.4 percent of newborns were born to single parents. The teen pregnancy rate is now dropping, but marital pregnancy and birth rates are also dropping, and nonmarital births to twenty-something parents remain high. Thus the percentage of babies born to single parents has remained at 1 in 3 for the last several years.

Some people think that this trend is characteristic of certain groups, such as different ethnic groups, a certain region of the country, or people at certain economic levels. But this trend is omnipresent. Consider my own community, Holland, Michigan, a relatively conservative Midwestern community. In 1960, 3 percent of babies born at Holland Community Hospital were born to unmarried parents. In 1997, 24 percent were born to unmarried parents. That's an eight-fold increase, roughly matching the six-fold increase nationally in the percentage of babies born to unmarried parents. Further, this is not just an American trend. These data are almost exactly the same as the data for the United Kingdom. Over this period, Britain has gone from 6 to 32 percent of babies born to single parents. So whatever the forces are that are driving these social trends, they cross Western cultures. But they're not in all cultures. In Japan in 1960, 1 percent of newborns were born to single parents. In 1997 the figure was still 1 percent.

This increase in the number of babies born to single parents is a very significant trend and has such great implications for your school districts that I want to unpack this a bit further. This six-fold

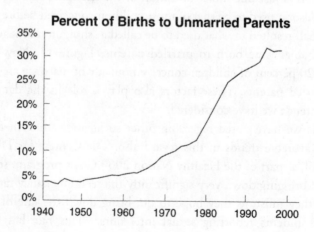

Figure 9.

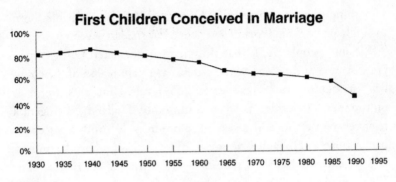

Figure 10.

increase in the percentage of babies born to unmarried parents reflects two realities: married parents are having fewer babies (this birth rate is half of what it was in 1960), and unmarried individuals are having more babies. It is the combination of these two factors that results in the data in Figure 9.

In the United States we have just crossed a very interesting line. It used to be that more than 4 in 5 first children were conceived within marriage. We have just reached a point where less than half of first children are conceived within marriage, as shown in Figure 10. The majority are now conceived outside of marriage.

This is just one more indication of the declining state of marriage. Also, it used to be that of those children conceived before marriage, half resulted in what used to be called a "shotgun marriage," so those babies were born to married parents, Figure 11. Now only about 20 percent of children conceived outside of marriage are born to married parents. These factors also play a role in the data and social trends we have considered.

As we have noted regarding other social indicators, there are some favorable trends in this regard also. The Centers for Disease Control, as part of the Healthy Nation 2000 Goals program, set the goal of bringing down very significantly the teen pregnancy rate. To do so they must, as they hope to do, bring down the rate of high school students reporting sexual intercourse. This rate has come down a little bit in the last few years.

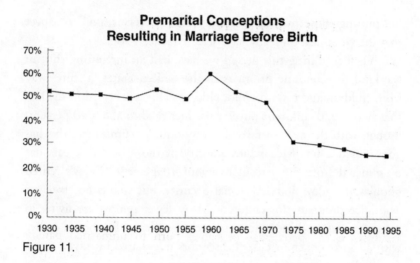

Figure 11.

Child abuse and neglect

Child abuse and neglect have become another aspect of the social recession. As Figure 12 indicates, there has been a huge increase, a five-fold increase, in the number of child abuse and neglect reports. In 1976, the first year these data were gathered, there were 600,000 such reports. Today there are about 3.1 million per year. The inevitable question is, is this a real increase in the victimization of children, or does that just represent increased sensitivity to, reporting of—even over reporting of—child abuse and neglect? I've asked this question of those who collect these data, and they tell me they can't precisely sort those things out. They think that about one-third of those cases are verifiable, documentable cases of real victimization of children. Further, we know that certain family structures are most often associated with child abuse and neglect. Most stepdads and live-in boyfriends are decent, caring guys. But a number of studies involving large samples have shown that the rate of child abuse and neglect and sexual misconduct is something on the order of ten times higher among live-in boyfriends and stepdads than among biological fathers and their children. Further, there are many more live-in boyfriends and stepdads than there were back in 1960.

So, putting those two facts together, there's every reason to expect that the victimization really has increased since 1960.

Further, during this period we have had an interesting shift in the kind of economic priorities in the United States, a shift away from children and toward senior citizens. This is reflected in the fact that since 1970 children's poverty has increased to about 20 percent, though with the current favorable economic circumstances this has gone down a bit. Meanwhile, poverty of those over 65 years has plummeted from 36 percent to about 10 percent. Today's retired population enjoys indexed Social Security, but this is not true for assistance programs for children. Many fewer seniors are living in poverty today, and most do not have dependents. Further, they live with all sorts of senior citizen discounts not shared by, say, a single mom taking her young child to a movie theater.

Depression

Data from a number of studies clearly indicate that marriage is not only good for the well-being of the children of that union but that married adults consistently report themselves happier when

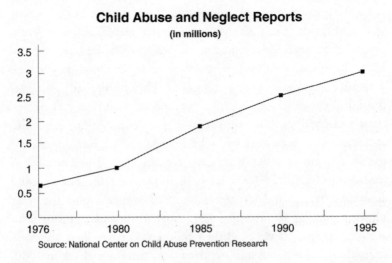

Figure 12.

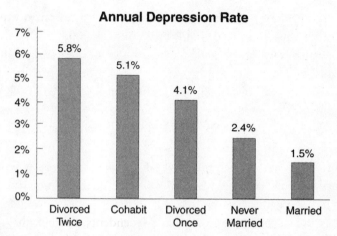

Annual Depression Rate

Figure 13.

married than when they were unmarried. Some important studies have also been done on the depression rate of people as a function of marital status. These data are summarized in Figure 13. Those divorced twice are more vulnerable to depression than those who are cohabiting who, in turn, are more vulnerable to depression than those divorced once. Those least likely to be depressed are those who remain in their first marriage. Of course it may be that those who are healthy and happy are more likely to get and stay married. But there also seem to be some physical and emotional benefits of a stable, committed, covenantal relationship between two adults who enduringly care for each other and are secure in that relationship.

However, the picture that emerges is that, despite the healthiness of marriage, marriage is in serious decline. We are marrying 3½ years later than back in 1960. Not only are people marrying later, they are marrying much less often. Many people are forsaking marriage, and of those who do, an increasing number are living together without marriage. In fact, only a slight majority of first marriages in the United States are not preceded by cohabitation. It used to be a kind of scandalous thing if it happened in your neighborhood. In 1960 in the United States, about 400,000 unmarried couples lived together (Figure 14); today 4.2 million do, representing 8.4 million

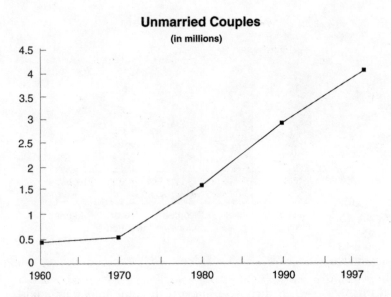

Unmarried Couples
(in millions)

Figure 14.

people. This also is a very dramatic cultural shift. Another way to view this is shown in Figure 15, which shows the percent of people who marry by age 25, as a function of when they reached age 25. In the late 1960s, 75 percent were married by age 25; by the late 1980s that was down to 50 percent. During this period the percent who were cohabiting was increasing to 40 percent. This study has now been redone with a more current sample, and we see a continuation of these trends.

Increased cohabitation undermines marriage for two reasons. First, it is an alternative to the binding commitments entailed by marriage. Second, even successful "trial marriages" tend to be predictive of divorce. (Marriages preceded by cohabitation fail more often, partly because people who cohabit are more accepting of divorce and partly because the experience of cohabitation strengthens the idea that marriage is often fragile and temporary.)

Consequences of these trends on children

The last question we will consider is whether there are consequences of these social trends for the well-being of children. We have

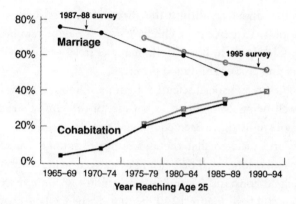

Figure 15.

noted that the well-being of children and youth is declining, and have seen that the health of marriage and the family has been in serious decline. Is there any connection between those two things? Does the health of children have anything to do with the health of families?

Consider first some simple economic data. Of the 20 percent of children who live in poverty, what kind of family structures are they in? As Figure 16 indicates, about half of children in single-parent

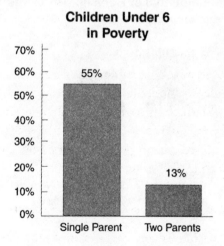

Figure 16.

families live under conditions the government describes as poverty, whereas only 13 percent of children in two-parent families live in poverty. Clearly there is a very dramatic correlation between family structure and risk of childhood poverty.

However, as a social scientist, I am more interested in the emotional well-being of children as a function of family structure. A number of studies have been completed that do control for economic status and race, so that the association of family structure with children's emotional well-being can be analyzed while economics and race are held constant. Census Bureau studies of more than 17,000 American children, Figure 17, show that the percentage of 3- to 17-year-olds who were treated for emotional behavioral problems in the past twelve months was about 9 percent for those living with a formerly married mother; 6½ percent for those living with a mother and stepfather; and less than 3 percent for those living with two biological parents. Children living with a mother and stepfather have problems at about the same rate as children living with a single parent. Sometimes people say, "Okay, kids in these disrupted families aren't doing as well, but it's all economics." The simplest way to dis-

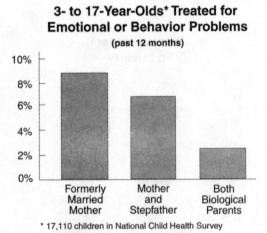

Figure 17.

pute this is to look at stepfamilies, for the economics are basically the same as those of intact biological-parent or adoptive families. A number of studies have been conducted on this issue, and all give the same pattern no matter what variable you look at, be it school truancy, juvenile delinquency, or emotional behavior problems.

A massive longitudinal study done in Britain involved virtually every child born in the first week of March 1958 in the United Kingdom—about 18,000 children. Through periodic interviews for more than 33 years, the lives of each of these persons has been carefully followed. This is an amazing study. Some interesting data emerged on the impact of divorce on children when it occurred between one interview and the next. Did the divorce have an effect on the children? It is often claimed that divorce is toxic for children only because it's symptomatic of the dysfunction and pathology that was pre-existing in that family, and which was already taking a toll on the children. But it turns out that before a divorce takes place, the children are doing nearly as well as the children whose parents are not about to divorce. After the divorce, these children show a decline in well-being, using all the normal measures. It's a quasi-experimental, but very significant, study. These issues are not a point of disagreement between Republicans and Democrats, liberals and conservatives. Hillary Rodham Clinton in her book *It Takes a Village,* Marion Wright Edelman in her book *The Measure of Our Success,* and James Dobson in his books share a common concern for the corrosion of the family and how it affects the well-being of children.

And yet having said this, I also think it's possible to overemphasize the direct effects of parents on children. The corrosion of the family may be affecting children by a more indirect route than the direct route of parental impact. I say this for several reasons. Considerable data has been gathered that challenges what is called *The Nurture Assumption,* to use the title of a recent book by Judith Rich Harris. This is a very challenging and very provocative book. The challenge to the nurture assumption comes from the fact that parental influence on personality is demonstrably small. We know this from two kinds of studies. One is the study of identical twins versus fraternal twins who were separated shortly after birth and reared separately, often without awareness of one another. We now have data on several hundred pairs of these very special people who share the same genes, but have been reared separately, sometimes in radically different circumstances. Studies show that these persons are astonishingly alike in their traits and characteristics, even their vulnerability to divorce as adults, which suggests that the home nurture of children has a limited impact on personality. Studies have also been done on adopted siblings who have different biological parents. Despite growing up in the same home environment, these adopted children are only slightly more alike in their personalities than any two children compared at random. They are somewhat more like their biological parents, whom they may never have met, but they are not much like them either.

So out of these studies, which are well-known to developmental psychologists and behavior geneticists, has come the conclusion that what is called the shared home environment seems not to be a potent shaper of children's personalities. However, their faith, their values, certain of their social behaviors, and ultimately their vocational interests are more demonstrably influenced by parental nurture.

For personality traits, about 50 percent of human variation is attributable to genetic factors. So what factors are involved in the other 50 percent if parental nurture is relatively small? One of the claims now made by Judith Rich Harris, among others, is that it is peer influence. Following are a few examples of the kind of data that point very strongly to peer influence. Consider an immigrant child who hears English spoken at home with one accent, and spoken with another accent in the neighborhood and at school. On growing up, whom will that child talk like? Will the child talk like the parents who provided home nurture, or will the child talk like the peers who provided the peer culture? Invariably the person will talk like the peers. Children play to an audience of their peers, the ones with whom they spend increasing amounts of time and in which they ultimately will find a mate. An evolutionary psychologist would say it makes sense that we are peer sensitive more than we are parent sensitive.

Here is another example. Let's say you're a young kid growing up and you have parents who smoke or don't, you have friends around you who smoke or don't. Is your smoking behavior going to be more reflective of your peers or your parents? Once again the answer is peers, not parents. This evidence is summarized in Judith Rich Harris's provocative, well-argued, and controversial book.

Some people have taken this conclusion as an attack on parents. Rather, in my judgment, it lightens the burden of guilt and judgment felt by many parents who have troubled children, who had been contaminated, if you will, by the toxic vapors seeping in from the culture, a culture that places blame largely on the parents, as well-meaning, well-intentioned, caring, and devoted as they may be. Further, this understanding may encourage teachers, youth ministers, boys and girls club volunteers, and school administrators to recognize the significance of their work with the peer culture. If you want to change kids, if you want to have an intervention program for youths, don't target individual children in isolation from their surrounding culture, target a whole school or a whole neighborhood. This should be the focus of your efforts and you should realize that what you're doing is very, very significant.

And as we think about the explosion in teen pregnancy, teen violence, teen depression, teen suicide, and realize that it's happening everywhere, does it really make sense to blame parents? Are parents not trying as hard as they used to? Or are parents struggling to swim upstream against a culture that seems to be pulling their children in a different direction? It is happening in Britain as well as in America. One of our greatest challenges is to understand the cultural influences that have shaped the values, the norms, the sexual ideas and behaviors that have become so prominent in contemporary society.

The Communitarian perspective

In response to these trends and concerns, a social renewal movement has been under way in the United States for the last several years that questions materialism and challenges individualism. An example is The Communitarian Network, co-founded by Amitai

Etzinoni, a recent president of the American Sociological Association, and William Galston, a speaker at the Van Andel Educators Institute last year, and who served as Domestic Policy Adviser for the first two years of the Clinton Administration. What the Communitarians are saying is that individual rights, important as they are, need to be held in balance with social responsibilities. We need to lift up the well-being of communities. We are not just isolated individuals; we're bonded with each other, and we need to care about those social connections. Thus the Communitarians are supportive of things like character education in schools as a way to strengthen shared moral values in communities, and thereby strengthen communities. Many Communitarians celebrate the place of faith, spirituality, and faith-based organizations in enhancing community life.

Another aspect of the social renewal movement is to challenge the media to take much greater responsibility for what they publish and produce for the public. There has been enormous research on the media's modeling of violence, and it has been confirmed that this tends to desensitize people to violence and lead to some imitated behavior that increases violence. There also is an indirect path by which the media can affect violence. The disintegration of families and the correlated cultural and peer effects of the cultural disintegration, such as cohabitation, nonmarital sexuality, and divorce, is also a source of increased violence. Do the media play a role in this disintegration? Many believe that the media's extensive modeling of impulsive sexuality contributes significantly to nonmarital sexuality, and to the disintegration of the family, and thus is an indirect route to increased violence. Thus, there are two ways in which the media put schools at increased risk for juvenile violence—directly by modeling violence and indirectly by modeling uncommitted sexuality. All of us, and particularly you as educators, need to think carefully, creatively, and wisely about these issues.

Individualism

Much has been written about individualism in America today. Cross-culture psychologists say that the United States is today the most individualistic nation in human history. But what I will focus on briefly are some of the popular ways in which we hear individualism expressed today as opposed to a more communal, collected way of thinking. We are individualistic in the way we talk. We say, "Do your own thing." "Seek your own bliss." "Challenge authority." "Celebrate your freedom." "If it feels good, do it." "Be true to yourself." "Shun conformity." "The highest morality is self-defined, so don't force your values on others." Values clarification is often cited as the ideal. But this clearly is a very individualistic idea. It is not about shared community values. Rather, in values clarification, what you need to do is understand who you are and clarify and strengthen your personal values.

Individualism can be expressed in various ways. "Avoid losing yourself in a co-dependent relationship where you're stuck with nurturing somebody else's dysfunction." "If you're going to love others, you've got to love yourself first." "Get in touch with yourself, trust your own intuition, prefer solo spirituality to collective spirituality." "Believe in yourself, be self-sufficient, and expect others to make it on their own likewise."

The overall emphasis in individualism is to assert your rights. So the ACLU on the left and the NRA on the right are both leaves off the same individualistic tree, asserting rights to own guns, sell pornography, and do business without regulations. It is all about upholding human freedom for the individual. In some cases it's freedom celebrated on the left, and other cases on the right. The Communitarians in the center want to raise questions about both extremes. These are matters of vital concern to you as educators and warrant careful thought and creative responses.

Faith and societal well-being

The final issue I will address is the relationship between faith and well-being, particularly societal well-being. In the last part of the 1990s there seems to be an increased interest in the culture in spirituality, broadly defined. A significant number of leading cultural commentators are talking about the spiritual poverty and spiritual

crisis of modern civilization. Various surveys are finding that materi-
alistic values are beginning to wane, with spiritual concerns increasing for relationships, nature, and the meaning of life. George Gallup
says one of the two dominant trends in society today is the search for
spiritual significance. A recent survey by the Gallup organization
reports that teens' interest in religion, particularly among male teens,
has increased discernibly since the late 1980s. And we see various
public displays of increased spiritual interest, such as the Million
Man March, Promise Keepers rallies, and the considerable interest in
angels. At one time recently, six of the ten best-selling books were on
spiritual themes of one sort or another. A marked interest in
Gregorian chants, movies with religious themes, and television that
has been touched by an angel has followed.

Is it true, as many people have supposed, that if people are connected to a religious community, they're less likely to behave in
socially dysfunctional ways? Several years ago, President Clinton said,
"If every kid in the neighborhood in America were in a religious
institution on weekends—a synagogue on Saturday, a church on
Sunday, a mosque on Friday—the drug rate, the crime rate, the violence rate, the sense of self-destruction would go way down. The
quality and character of this country would go way up." Is this true?
Many politicians are embracing what is currently a very popular
theme, to engage faith-based institutions in dealing with social problems in America. Are they right? Is there any connection between
faith and the social health of the nation? Voltaire, an atheist, said, "I
want my attorney, my tailor, my servants, even my wife, to believe in
God.... Then I shall be robbed and cuckolded less often."

There are a number of areas of research that relate religious
faith and faith communities to social health, and the results give
some support of what politicians are saying about faith-based communities. We know, for example, that actively religious people are
much less likely, on the order of half as less likely, to be juvenile
delinquents, abuse drugs and alcohol, divorce, and commit suicide.
We know from studies in other countries that actively religious people—Jews in Israel, Catholics in the Netherlands and in Spain, the
Orthodox in Greece, and Protestants in Germany—are all less

hedonistic and self-oriented in their expressed values than are their irreligious country people. We also know that where churchgoing is high in the United States, crime rates are relatively low. So you can much more comfortably leave your car unlocked in Provo, Utah, than in my economically similar hometown of Seattle, Washington, as indexed by crime rates in those two communities.

What about faith and altruism? A number of studies done in the 1950s and 1960s that relate religion and prejudice found that religious church members, especially the conservative church members, expressed a measure of religious prejudice. However, among church members, those who attended faithfully and regularly expressed less prejudice than those who attended only occasionally and seemed nominal in their commitment. We also know that during the 1960s, clergy were much less prejudiced than were their laity, and it was clergy who provided much of the driving energy for the civil rights movement in the United States.

There are some interesting but little known facts regarding religion and generosity with money. Who gives away money in the United States to charitable causes? Those who do not attend church or synagogue give about ½ percent of their income to charitable purposes. Among occasional attendees, the rate is about 1½ percent, and among weekly attendees it is about 3 percent. Thus, even though the latter group falls far short of tithing, there is a very significant correlation between religiosity and charitableness. In fact, George Gallup, Jr., in a national survey on charitable giving and volunteerism, done for Independent Sector and funded by the Kellogg Foundation and others, reported that the 24 percent of Americans who attend church or synagogue weekly give 48 percent of all charitable contributions; the other three-fourths of Americans give the other half of the money.

And who is volunteering? Those who say religion is not very important to them volunteer at half the rate of those who say religion is very important. Thus, there is clear evidence that an active religious faith has a positive impact on people when it comes to donating their money and time.

Historically we can also look at who founded universities, who promoted literacy, who promoted abolition here in the United States, who led the civil rights movements in the United States and South Africa, and who first brought medicine and hospitals to the Third World. Clearly those with strong religious convictions played major roles in all these endeavors. So once again we can see that although religion has sometimes been a rationale for great injustice and brutality, it has, on balance, in Western culture been associated with many successes in education, humanitarian efforts, and social reform. Indeed, going on right now in the United States are a number of faith-based efforts to further social reform and social-healing processes, and to lift up and nurture individuals who are in stress circumstances. One of the significant issues before us as a nation is the extent to which the United States government should provide funding support to these "faith-based" initiatives, with the contingent requirement that those funds are not used for parochial purposes. If a faith-based drug intervention program is more successful at getting people off the streets and off drugs, should it be given government funding in competition with other initiatives? Or because it is faith-related, does that violate the separation of church and state? This issue will continue to be debated.

As educational leaders, you are well aware that these cultural trends are driving people to parochial schools, to charter schools, and even to home schools. For those of you who are in public education, as my own children have been, this is the world in which you live. The challenges facing you are great. The work you and your colleagues are doing is tremendously important for today's youth and tomorrow's America. Take heart that America is awakening to the great American paradox and that, with renewed core values, better times may lie ahead.

William Johnson
Professor Emeritus of
Landscape Architecture
Former Dean
School of Natural Resources
University of Michigan

A landscape architect by training, William Johnson has pioneered the development and use of integrative processes whereby human needs are addressed in the context of particular environments, both natural and cultural.

In his work on projects of urban design, campus and regional planning, natural resource management, and historic preservation, he seeks to balance social, cultural, and environmental factors.

A graduate of Michigan State University, he received his master's degree from Harvard University.

William Johnson

Chapter 9

Community Building—
New Insights from an Old Art

As I have spent time with you these last two days, I realized that you, as teachers and school administrators, are my heroes. I find it amazing that anyone can sustain such creativity, motivation, and skill in working with the children and young people of today. While I applaud everything I've been hearing here, I empathize with your aches, your pains, and your difficulties. It makes my Michigan dean-ship days seem like a walk in the park. When I hear about problems in the schools of Chicago, Newark, and Atlanta, I realize I have noth-ing to add. I'm not in your field. I'm in a very different field. In my time with you I will strive to go to the center of my field to talk about some issues, with the expectation that we will discover some inter-esting crossovers to your work and the issues you face. Two crossovers that I'm sure will emerge are: the concept and phenomena of com-munity building, and the process by which we plan.

Everything you do, whether it's intended or not, has something to do with building up or tearing down the community in which your schools exist. It may be that in the past there has been a hands-off tradition between the schools and that community, but I think it's a different day. I will say, as strongly as I can, that if there is any institution that can have an impact on making more livable commu-nities for the future of this country, it is our schools. This is where the kids are, this is where the parents are, and this is where the hearts are. I see great potential in our schools for real support and advoca-cy for developing better communities. Given that, let me see if I can connect with you. I am used to talking with people in my own field, using our own professional jargon, but I will do my best to make mutually rewarding crossovers.

The other crossover from my field to yours is the planning process, which will be the focus of my second lecture. I will explain the planning process by telling you the story of this community (Holland, Michigan) and the renewal of its downtown. That renewal was a major victory and probably is one of the most exciting such stories in this country. It is the story of people who had the will to combine both public and private money to restore a broken downtown, broken not so much physically but in terms of being competitive in the marketplace. In anticipation of that lecture, and as a background for my comments on community building, some introductory remarks on how I approach the planning process may be helpful.

My business involves the process of thinking about creating places. I am oriented to physical form and the environment as a physical place. The elements I use in planning physical spaces are

crucial in thinking about the form that a community ought to take. These elements are shown on the following diagram.

Framework thinking

Essential to achieving an appropriate result is a "vision." Our community-building endeavor must be directed toward what we aspire to accomplish. As we think about shaping that vision, certain problems, obstacles, challenges, and opportunities emerge. One must know as much as possible about the place and the people who will live, work, or have activities in that place. This may involve exploring the cultural history, the history of the place, and the overall environment. You look at each of these areas with the expectation of discovering new insights, and suddenly a plethora of ideas start falling on the table. It never fails. Strategies begin to emerge, strategies that are essential in achieving the vision.

I do not place these elements in a linear pattern. I have not said one's first, one's second, and one's third, although you tend to do a bit of this. The order has to do more with the notion that they all relate, and there's no particular moment, order, or time when they have to interrelate. One thing spawns another.

Our normal processes tend to be somewhat rigid. They don't allow the agility necessary to work quickly and creatively, and therefore the efforts we undertake to plan and look ahead tend to be expensive and time-consuming. After you finish such a planning effort, you don't want to do it again. It requires too much energy. The result: planning gets put on the shelf.

The process I have described becomes a kind of engine, a reciprocal engine. It doesn't matter where you start the process. You can start with understanding the people, with some new ideas, with a fresh vision, or with a new problem that pops up. Any one of these issues can become the motivating force that starts the engine. Once the engine starts, the process cycle starts. As long as you keep the engine running—keep it cycling—the process continues feeding back new insights. But if the process becomes linear, the engine stops cycling. You have reached the status quo of that moment and the dynamics of the process stop.

The cyclic nature of this process is of great benefit, for with it come speed, brevity, and a quickness. There is nothing more tiring in the planning process than to get bogged down in information over-load or, almost the opposite, a lack of the ideas that should be pop-ping up quickly.

The fundamental process here is one of "scoping," and it's best when done quickly. What is scoping? When you scope, you look for ... search for ... discover ... react ... move on. It's quick. I tell the story of Holland because it is a classic example of all these things being present—not in highly formal ways but inherently in the way the community works.

The length of time this process takes can be the same as any planning effort, but by the time I finish planning a project, everyone involved has gone through the cycle many times. Every dimension has been checked. Every idea has been measured against the vision. Does it fit the vision? I like ideas to come up early in the process. Ideas that come up early go through the cycle several times. Producing ideas early in the game is an important feature of an ite-grative process. It leads to a concept I call "framework thinking." Framework thinking says that you don't need to define too much of the future at the outset. You need only to define the essentials that "run the engine." Let the flesh be added when the time is appropri-ate, when time allows, and when you are ready to move ahead.

Community building

What do I mean when I talk about community building? It too is a process. Community building implies making plans. It implies vision. It implies investment. It implies work. It's an art, not a sci-ence. It is an art that was very familiar to our forefathers when they began to settle this country and build their communities. The process did not have a name as such. But it did occur.

Community building embraces all the parts of growing a com-munity. A community is an organism in flux. It embraces concerns about identity, about sense of place, about pride of place—all very important terms. When you're proud of your place, you protect your place. Community has to do with roots. It has to do with security, with safe places. It has to do with diversity and choices. It has to do with connectedness, which leads to wholeness.

Many of our communities are broken communities—unconnected bits and pieces of development. They're not whole. They hurt, and they hurt us. People in these communities are seemingly satisfied with the status quo, unaware that there is a way to have a better kind of community.

I want to mention a couple of ideas I heard from other speakers. To me, these ideas are significant. The phrase "the best of times, and the worst of times" has been mentioned more than once. It is true. These are fantastic times. But sometimes when I look ahead and see the terrible pain that is coming for kids, and the choices they must make, I wish I were living in an earlier time. I agonize about television and street crimes. These are indeed the best of times and the worst—all at the same time.

The other idea discussed here that I like is that of "loose connections." Involvement is crucial to effective community building. The vertical relationships referred to in the earlier lecture truly are essential. One of the great difficulties in this country, in terms of looking ahead, is that our thinking tends to be compartmentalized. We're taught to understand things in pieces. Universities compartmentalize teaching and learning. In general, more is known about taking things apart than putting things together. In community planning, we tend to allow various uses to remain unconnected. We don't seem to mind. But this lack of connectivity hurts.

My beginning in getting excited about life was in early high school. And that excitement began with art. I was the one who had a little studio near the third floor stairway, where I made all the charts and cartoons for those running for office. I was the local artist. But the notion of art for art's sake was not exciting to me. Then one day, in 1947, as I walked through a hallway exhibition on the Michigan State College campus, I saw colorful portrayals of case studies wherein problems of our society were being solved with artistic endeavors

... a process called "design." To me, that was art at work! It thrilled me, and I became a landscape architect. Landscape architecture combined my father's and my grandfather's work (engineering and tool-making) with my sense of art. I loved the idea of combining engineering with art then, and I still do today.

Here's an important thought that I want to present to you as leaders and administrators in education. Your educational mission, with the overall vision you have and the communication systems that are open to you, is so basic to community life that I think the school systems of America could be powerful advocates for more livable communities. I'm not suggesting that school systems become caretakers of the community or even inventors of community, but rather proponents for a better community. How can a school system influence its community, have an influence on making a community more livable and more supportive? I suggest that your school-to-community relationships be more on the proactive side, rather than merely reactive.

The problem I'm trying to convey to you has to do with a hurting urban world. James Kunstler puts this quite well in his book *Home from Nowhere: Remaking Our Everyday World for the Twenty-First Century*. His diagnosis is excellent. I understand what he is saying in his rather sharp and at times harsh way, particularly when he says that we used to know how to build communities. He says that we have left the towns that we invented so inspirationally and, by way of societal realities, we have created a suburban world in which we find a sense of community missing. He views suburbia as the *nowhere* in his book title. *Home,* he very powerfully implies, is where we once lived in generations past, when we seemed to know how to put people together with their places in a more sensitive and whole way. He is trying to figure out what the new "somewheres" are and how they can be achieved. He advocates the "new urbanism" movement as the solution. I'm not so sure about that part of his book. I think new urbanism is one of the solutions, but I believe there are other approaches as well.

I want to emphasize these points through two stories illustrated with slides. One story is about a neighborhood of modest homes, located on the edge of a city, that was being proposed for a shopping center location, and how it was instead restored and renewed by timely design intervention. The other is a story about building "someplace" in a suburban "nowhere."

But first, let me cite three basic contemporary mindsets that have a negative impact on our efforts to build strong communities. The first is the "I want it now" syndrome, involving short-term investment cycles and the need for immediate results. Why do we so often think in terms of four years when it takes thirty years to achieve some things in a healthy way? This short-term mindset is a major problem when we are trying to think creatively about long-term community development.

The second mindset is the tendency to favor *extensive* development over *intensive* development. This extensive development frame of mind probably stems from the mobility afforded us by the automobile and a seemingly endless supply of relatively cheap land. If one place wears out or becomes too crowded, we don't solve the problems, we move. Rather than working within the older community, we simply move out a bit farther to design new places.

Third, and perhaps the most damaging of our mindsets, is that we tend to be single-purpose oriented without any sense of responsibility to integrate one purpose with another. You are in your present position for a single purpose. Your organization has a single mission. That singular focus consumes most of your time and energy. An example is a state Department of Transportation. It has a single purpose—to build roads—and that purpose is accomplished with great skill. Not central to the mission of the road builders is the impact those roads have on the quality of community life. When you consider that most other parts of a community are single-purpose oriented as well, you can understand why our communities are not as livable as we might like.

One of the books that inspired me as a young professional in the early '60s was John Gardner's *Excellence: Can We Be Equal and Excellent Too?* Gardner noted that the problems of society affect every part of a university. I hadn't realized that before. He was pointing out that universities don't provide as much reward for inter-disciplinary work as they do for deepening a single body of knowledge. Given this early learning pattern, there is a tendency for us to continue to understand our world in pieces without enough understanding of it as a set of interdependencies.

I have been drawn to the challenge of interdisciplinary work, for effective design and planning is an inherently integrative process.

Quality of place

There is a direct relationship between the qualities of neighborhood and qualities of community. I grew up in a neighborhood on the south side of Lansing, Michigan, in the late '30s and early '40s. I could walk downtown in ten minutes. My playground was the alley. I love alleys. There was a certain garage roof on that alley where we gathered. The neighbors didn't seem to mind, and we had a nice view down the alley. I knew every kitchen in the block. I knew every housewife. They were my friends' mothers. One year my dad built a full-sized airplane in the basement, piece by piece. He then broke out a section of the wall to get the bigger parts out of the basement. All that summer he worked on that airplane in the backyard.

Because of that airplane, our backyard became the "central square" for the neighborhood. All summer there were crowds of kids in our backyard. We didn't have a playground, but there was an empty lot down the way where we played ball once in a while, and every six weeks or so one of the dads would mow it. Because our neighborhood had a strong sense of place for me, my view of the larger community was very positive.

My future algebra teacher, Miss Taylor, lived in the next block. I'll never forget her because she was, to me, a very severe woman. Her gray hair was done in a tight bun. She wore tiny little glasses, and she could look right through a stone wall. I knew I was going to have her for algebra in high school. My older brother and sister had already taken her math courses, and they had come back with pretty frightening stories. I was scared to death.

In Miss Taylor's backyard was the best grape arbor in town. She also had two pear trees, an apple tree, and a peach tree. I knew each one and I knew where I could get through the fence. I delighted in slipping in at night to take bunches of grapes and share them with my buddies in the alley. The grapes were especially delicious because they were Miss Taylor's grapes!

One summer we were out of town for a couple weeks, and on our return my mother got a call from Miss Taylor. "How's Billy? Is he OK?" she asked.

My mother explained that I had been away.

"Well, he hasn't been in the grape arbor lately," Miss Taylor told my mother, "and I wondered if everything was OK."

My future algebra teacher! Knew about my nocturnal visits to her grape arbor! A couple years later, when I walked into her algebra class, I naturally was very apprehensive. But Miss Taylor, who I did not yet know was a great teacher, looked at me and smiled. This severe woman smiled at *me,* of all people!

I wasn't very good at math at first, but I worked harder in algebra that first year than I had ever worked before. From then on, I got all A's—first in algebra, then in trigonometry, and finally in calculus.

That one forgiving smile did the trick.

My neighborhood was about relationships—a community. That's what towns were meant to be when they were built in the early days of America. Towns back then were artfully conceived and built with relationships in mind. They were meant to be places where Miss Taylor was not only my algebra teacher but also a person who was watching over me, who cared about me. My positive attitude about the important relationship between people and place was formed in those few neighborhood years, when I was a boy. I think about the neighborhoods that kids grow up in today. How many have the good qualities that I experienced?

Neighborhoods come in all different shapes and sizes. That doesn't matter. What does matter to the kids growing up there is for the neighborhood to have a close-knit set of relationships. These relationships, these interdependencies, do so much to set up a sense of great pride in community later on. Effective community building is all about building relationships and recognizing our interdependencies.

Planning ahead in a changing world

Knowing how to manage change is essential to making effective plans. Community building is a moving target, and therefore I believe it's a shapeable target. If it's moving, it's dynamic; it's not a set piece. The same must be true in the field of primary and secondary education. That's why I say to you that your influence could be a powerful factor in advocating for better communities, just as you so effectively advocate for better education.

Many in this country feel that planning is too prescriptive. They don't like its constraining and controlling nature, so they don't do it. There is no national plan, no state plans, and few regional plans. Generally, city and town plans are becoming more and more minimal. For many, that is the idea—the intent. They want to keep the marketplace open and dynamic so every possible gain can be had from private initiatives. In this way one can remain flexible and opportunistic in the face of the many imponderables of the future. This makes sense when the planning process is ponderous and slow. But when planning is done with a "vision," the end result can be dynamic and inspirational.

History tells us that we are able to plan ahead with great skill. Our forefathers did it, as evidenced by the many villages and towns built with thoughtful, motivated, and highly skilled craftsmanship. Holland is such a town. Back then, planning was not considered an interference with free enterprise. And back then, as now, Americans were pretty independent. They saw their cooperative efforts—working together—as a part of their independence.

Planning isn't the problem; the problem is the kind of planning we do. We should not stop planning because it's heavy, burdensome, time-consuming, and full of challenges. That's not the issue. The issue is to find a way to make planning quick, factual, and discovery-oriented. That's the kind of planning we need. Of the many issues that impact planning in contemporary society, I want to emphasize three:

One is "the automobile." It seems to be our nemesis. Over the last century, we've been persuaded to count on two assumptions. The first is that we have an endless supply of developable land. The other is that the only way to move about is by rubber-tired automobile. We opted out of any mass-transportation system years ago, and there is no population density in this country that promises to support extensive mass-transit systems. We are, in fact, fully committed to the automobile. It is a love/hate relationship that seriously damages our ability to build truly livable communities.

The second issue is "population growth." The sheer numbers of people we face in this country represent enormous issues. You know the statistics better than I do. I don't know what we're going to do about the growth curve. We seem to assume we will solve the problem if and when it arises. It is disconcerting to realize that there is no particular strategy before us. My hope is that we become seriously concerned about how we can preserve and build the effective communities of the twenty-first century.

My third point is "mobility." The problem of mobility isn't just automobiles; it's everything having to do with the ability to be in one place while operating in another. Consider "cyberspace." This kind of electronic mobility is one more sample of "the best of times, and the worst of times" mentioned earlier. When is it a plus, and when is it a minus? It can be both. I think we have to rethink the meaning of neighborhood, the meaning of centrality, the meaning of proximity, and maybe even the meaning of community. These traditional qualities may even need new definitions.

But if we are responsible about understanding the relationship between people and places, and make the planning process more dynamic, new and intriguing insights about the future can occur. I will demonstrate a sample of this approach in the second lecture when I describe a bit of the story of Holland's downtown.

Prospects for the future

Some recent innovations on the planning front show great promise. One is a return to more compact development; pulling our communities into tighter development centers. Communities across the country are beginning to prove that this can be done effectively. Another promising direction is a more creative mix of uses. Kunstler makes a dramatic point of how our zoning laws and the standards with which we control development are in fact producing the "nowhere" he speaks of in his book. Most Americans believe that the best way to preserve open land is to have large-lot zoning. But, ironically, such zoning actually quickens and extends the impact of development on open space. A home on a five- to twenty-acre lot takes that land out of its highest and best use potential and scatters development disturbance much farther than tighter development patterns would do. The more effective way to preserve open space is to bring homes together and find mechanisms to manage productively the open land areas. We can build better communities, and people throughout the country are already increasing their efforts to do so. Along with the trend toward a more dynamic planning process, the move toward more compact development and a more creative mix of uses are all very promising innovations.

I want to tell you two stories that demonstrate the principles I've just described.

The first involves the restoration of a residential neighborhood—Garden Homes—that was about to disappear and become a shopping center. My happening upon this scene was serendipity; I just bumped into it. Amazingly, in just three years this slum-condition neighborhood was totally renewed.

As I was working with this neighborhood, I was also working on some Detroit neighborhood preservation teams. But the complexity of the city's neighborhood issues was so overwhelming and the bureaucracy so dominant, there seemed no way to get freshness and creativity into Detroit's neighborhood renewal system.

This situation—the neighborhood destined to become a shopping center and the Detroit neighborhood preservation effort—was a parallel moment that emphasized the difference in the two locations.

In the first, the neighborhood slated to be a shopping center, we were able to get a hold of it and introduce some creativity. The people who lived there geared up and salvaged their neighborhood. It was a grassroots effort. My role was simply as coach.

The Detroit neighborhoods did not change. They remain as they were.

Restoring a neighborhood

This story involves a little community within the city of Ann Arbor, Michigan. If you know Ann Arbor, you really can't fathom the slum conditions that existed there. The community is on the edge of town, near an interchange with a main artery into the city. The place was plotted in the 1920s with rather large, one- to two-acre lots, sort of rural in development. You've seen such areas around cities. The city of Ann Arbor had annexed all the area around this community, but there was no sewer service, no city water. It was easy pickings for a developer to come in and say, "This worn-out ninety-home subdivision would be a perfect spot for a strip shopping center." This happens all the time, but fortunately we caught this one just in time.

I was leaving the office after working late one evening when a social worker I knew, Lori, walked in the door. She was exhausted and in tears. She had just left a neighborhood meeting. She had been working for a couple years in this subdivision, trying to figure out some way to fend off the developer while the community got itself together to determine its future. Through her tears she told me that it was over. The group she was working with had said that it was no use to continue the effort. The developer had made an offer to each of the ninety families, and everybody seemed willing to sell. The tragedy was that there was no place for most of these people to go. They had modest homes, and there were few homes in Ann Arbor that they could afford to buy, and not many in the region. This was a defining moment in terms of keeping this modest little neighborhood intact.

I agreed to talk with the group and walked back with her to the neighborhood. The group had not yet left the basement where they were meeting. I asked if they were willing to lead the effort to save their community, rather than having Lori or me or somebody else from outside the neighborhood take charge. They declined. They said they were tired of it all and didn't know how to begin or what to do next. They had never done anything like this before.

"Do these folks truly want to leave? Do they want to sell out?" I asked.

They weren't sure. Some said neighbors did want to sell, but others said they weren't sure. In public they were saying one thing, in private they said another.

So I agreed to take two months and work with them, no fee, if they would do one thing: circulate a confidential questionnaire about every resident's willingness to stay or leave. That's all I wanted to know. Lori had been working with some University of Michigan people who had a questionnaire already designed. We got that out to the residents, got the responses, and a month later, we gathered in my office in Ann Arbor with the whole community—about 150 people.

The results of that survey indicated that almost every person wanted to keep that community intact. They did not, in fact, want to sell out to the developer. So I said, "Given that, you must have the desire to accomplish this. So let's go—you lead and Lori and I will coach." In spite of their reticence at taking the lead, a few stepped forth and agreed to learn how. So began the work, and the most amazing things happened.

It is important to understand the reality of what we started with. People in Ann Arbor were afraid of this community because it had every appearance of a slum. Although the area was actually a pretty nice place, some of the conditions were scary. When it rained, the roads would go to deep mud. Abandoned houses were a problem. The homes were not connected to the city's sewer system. People had outhouses, and in places there was raw sewage in the streets. It is hard to imagine, even today, that this was in Ann Arbor just a few years ago, not far from the famous "big house" stadium of the University of Michigan.

Slated to become a shopping mall, this Ann Arbor community had abandoned houses, deeply rutted roads, and small homes on big lots with
outhouses because of the lack of city sewer and water lines.

To solve the sewage problem, I went to every home and asked
the residents if they could afford to hook up to sewer and water. Half
of them could, half could not. We needed supplemental funds—a
block grant and matching city funds. After the committee reviewed
a conceptual plan for the renewal and restoration of the neighborhood, a confidential financial plan was worked out with every household to hook up to sewer and water, using as much as possible of
their own capital. It took a lot of work to prepare ninety different
negotiations. I was involved with almost all of them. Some who had

large lots but limited funds platted their property to sell one, two, and even three lots to raise the funds.

During the process an interesting fact surfaced about the quality of the place. Some of the folks were observing that even though their community was within walking distance of junior high and elementary schools, their children did not have a place to play—they felt they had no park. Recalling my neighborhood alley experiences, it occurred to me that this neighborhood, in spite of its rag-tag conditions, most likely was a great place for kids. I asked the parents to bring their kids along the next Saturday. We would follow them through their "playground." About a dozen kids came, and they showed us where they played. I made a map of every spot in the neighborhood where they took us. It was a great, great place to play. They had trees to climb, fences to hop over, trails to follow, and garage roofs to sit on to observe life around them. They knew each place by name. Every favorite tree had a name. There were stories about them. Most property owners were aware of the kids' travels and were tolerant. Most parents didn't know how their kids played. But these kids had a "park" that was better than any park in Ann Arbor. With a few basic modifications we built that basic "park," along with its stories, into the new "official" park of the new plan.

The natural "park" where neighborhood kids played
needed only a few changes.

With that experience, residents began to get excited about the prospects for their neighborhood. This was not only a great place to live but also a place worthy of some creative design effort.

During one of our early sessions I prepared a simple chalk diagram of a concept for the "new" old place. Using what the kids had shown us, the plan included a central piece of green that was, in part, low, oft-flooded land with trails connecting to the streets. Some of the new houses were oriented in clusters to the central green and to the old streets. Throughout the planning process we used this diagram as a vision. It was the basic idea for the community.

With the plan in hand, the resident committee started in with great energy. They applied for and received a federal block grant and matching support from the city of Ann Arbor. Each family contributed a share of private capital as well. Within two years the project entered the construction phase, and in another year a ribbon-cutting ceremony occurred. The original developer with the strip shopping center idea came back and developed a little "pocket" retail center, which is now part of the neighborhood.

The transformation of this Ann Arbor neighborhood was a kind of private-public partnership that worked out very well. It began humbly and remained modest. That is its strength today. It is now

New homes were built in "clusters," connected by pathways to the rest of the Garden Homes community.

one of the most desirable places to live in the city. Out of the ninety original families, only two left, but more than a dozen new families moved in. That's the statistic I'm most proud of.

From this experience I would stress two things. One is the "will" to do something about one's convictions. The basic question is, do you truly want to get well? If the answer is yes, you probably will get well. The residents found the motivation to achieve a clear objective—to keep the neighborhood sound. It simply could not have been done without the will.

The second point I want to stress is the "integrative process" by which we worked. We went quickly, simply, and easily through a process of thinking from vision to detail, again and again. Through a frequent reiteration of relating information, ideas, and their implications, the next steps were always self-evident. The residents, by doing the work, took ownership of the plans and were thereby inspired to make things happen. I was only a coach.

Prairie Crossing

The other story is a more recent one. It involves a new community, Prairie Crossing, north of Chicago. Its distinctive feature is its tight clustering of homes around a distinctive central green, which otherwise would have been developed in a typically anonymous subdivision pattern. The intent was to preserve approximately 2,500 acres of agricultural land in perpetuity while developing a small and distinctive residential community. It involved marketplace purchases by public and private entities, township and county restrictions, as well as private easements and deed restrictions. Like my first example, it is a story about the will to achieve an inspired vision. The eventual name of the community became "Prairie Crossing," recalling the natural history of the original great Midwestern prairies and the cultural history of two major rail lines crossing at the western edge of the site.

The key advocates for this project were the Donnellys— Gaylord Donnelly and his wife, Dot—both exceptional people. They loved the rural countryside in that part of Chicago. They wanted to

Prairie Crossing, north of Chicago, was designed for clusters of homes built around a central green.

preserve farmland, but they knew development was inevitable. The Donnelleys purchased the site, located north of Chicago near Libertyville in central Lake County, to assure low-density development and preserve rural character. The only downside was that this removed the mixed-use development category and made it residential. Well intended as it was, we struggled with this constraint later in the planning process in the interests of creating a more substantive center.

It has now been about twelve years since I was invited to be involved in the Prairie Crossing planning process. Even though the process has been long and arduous, an indication of its success is that current development phases are sold out. For those who have been drawn to live at Prairie Crossing, it has meant buying into a lifestyle, not just a home.

Layout of the land

The Des Plaines River, along with its many forest preserves, runs north and south on the west side of Chicago, parallel to the Lake Michigan shoreline. Farther to the west is the Fox River Valley. These two north-south drainage basins constitute the major drainage patterns in the northern Chicago suburbs. Gaylord Donnelly's concept was to somehow build a community that would be in harmony with agriculture. As we gathered one day to work with the county, I saw on the table of one of the county planning officials a well-worn little diagram. In studying the diagram, it was apparent that some discussions had occurred in the past regarding the possibility of an east-west open-space system that would complement the north-south open space of the Des Plaines River and connect the Des Plaines to the Fox River. I picked up the diagram and added it to our conceptual considerations.

That diagram became a kind of vision. No one seemed to think this idea was quite achievable. But we plugged it into our thinking about the site for the new village and its surrounding open space. We thought about the village as part of a major open-space corridor that might someday extend from the Des Plaines River to the Fox River. It was, for many, quite inspirational to think that big.

The challenge was to bring together all the privately owned properties that were needed to make this happen. Over the next three to four years, I spent a good deal of time working with about twenty landowners in the vicinity of the site with the intent to establish a broad base of private support for protecting rural character. I met with each family, asking about their plans for the future. In due time I knew each family quite well, and they shared with me some of their expectations for their land. Most were interested in keeping the rural quality in concert with low-density residential development for the long term. They had considered in the past home sites here and there on their property, and they showed me such locations. It took about three years, but we worked out an agreed-upon density for about twenty different parcels. In assembling those twenty parcels into an overall plan, the resulting density was light enough to think of an area of nearly 2,000 acres as an open-space system. Owners' commitments were set forth in home site locations and certain public pathway easements. We located a major public pathway as part of a regional trail system through the community connecting to the Des Plaines River.

One key step was to work with the owners of a neighboring landfill so that they would finish out their landfill in a harmonious way. This landfill is now in the process of becoming a regional park as a fitting neighbor to Prairie Crossing. Some of the revenue from the expansion of the landfill has been allocated to the support of the open-space system. So even waste-management techniques have been integrated with community design to achieve a unique development character.

In the plan for Prairie Crossing, the homes were clustered in a drainage basin defined by two old hedgerows, typical of Midwest rural character. The hedgerows were used to align paths and service lanes, and the drainage basin suggested the digging of a small lake like so many in the area. The old farmstead has been preserved as the center of an organic farming initiative. Two young couples have been hired as the organic growing experts, and they produce vegetables and fruits, not only for the community residents at an annual subscription rate but also for an area-wide Saturday market. In many ways this is a return to the spirit of prairie life.

On the larger preserve, a half-acre piece of original prairie—never touched by a plow—was found. That half acre contained more than 100 species of prairie grass, and not one weed. Much of the open space not being farmed, including much of the landfill regional park, will be returned to the same mix of prairie grasses.

The village of Prairie Crossing was established to provide housing while preserving farmland on the nearly 2,000-acre site.

In the new homes there is an attempt to bring back some of the character of the farmhouse architecture. The houses are quite close together, with an attractive central green a key feature of the total design. The bankers at first were skeptical of the small lots because this part of suburban Chicago features large lots and substantial homes. Now the sense is that they are enthusiastic about the quality and attractiveness of the Prairie Crossing lifestyle.

Prairie Crossing is truly a "connected" place, giving the sense that each element is part of the whole plan. You can get on a local pathway that connects to Wisconsin by way of the Des Plaines River. Two barns and an old schoolhouse from the area were brought to the site to set up the unique character of the village center. A charter school is being considered. A barn-raising event was a feature of the village-center building process.

Prairie Crossing is beginning to be a place of strong identity and a great place in which to raise a family, center one's professional life, or shift to a quieter lifestyle. Even though it is technically a subdivision, it clearly is not an anonymous piece of the suburbs.

Some final thoughts

I wanted to share these two slide-illustrated stories to demonstrate the importance of integrated thinking in community development. The first story of the Garden Homes subdivision restoration showed how the residents became energized by understanding how a creative process relating a vision to everyday realities produces new insights on how to make things happen. The story of Prairie Crossing is an example of how an overall open-space vision drove a simple need for new suburban homes into a village concept where each part of the community energized another.

I can't help thinking about school systems in the same way. A community is made up of many parts, and a school system is a major one. We're familiar with the manner in which a sound community plan provides the framework for an effective school system. But it can work the other way, too—a creative notion about how kids learn and teachers teach can drive the way a community is shaped.

As we think of the future I hope that there will be an increasing inclination to be more integrative about community building and not so single-purpose oriented.

I think about how school locations can be such a strong place-making power.

I think about how kids ought to be able to move from home to school in easier and less automobile-dependent ways.

I think of how important school sites are in not only providing recreation but also in teaching kids about the natural world and local cultural history.

I think of how the open-space linkages of an interconnected local school system could provide a more positive framework for neighborhood design than our suburban mindset allows.

Such school-community relationships once were more influential than it seems they are now. I sense it is time to give them fresh interpretation in the days to come.

William Johnson

Chapter 10

Designing Memorable Place—
Relating Vision to Action

During the two days I have been with you, I have been impressed with the range of issues you are discussing. I'm picking up some interesting insights. Still very much a learner, I find this experience extremely refreshing. I particularly resonate with some of the concepts David Myers presented in his lecture.

One of these is the idea of "thin slices" of behavior. It is "thin slices" I will be talking about later when I speak of planning cycles that are short, quick, and frequent. They are not meant to displace a planning process with something that is less than needed in terms of length and time, for I believe extensive data and thorough analyses are essential to responsible planning. But many times the process can become so ponderous in its lineality that it can dull what otherwise would be inspired thought. I am going to use the "thin slice" term in the future because it's a helpful descriptor of my cyclic approach to planning and design.

Another thing I found very encouraging in David's talk is a note of optimism in regard to contemporary society that I often worry and wonder about. I'm curious about his "self-correcting" theory in view of the need for substantial change regarding our societal ills. Maybe things will go so far and become so illogical that society will find the need for a course change self-evident. I don't sense this tendency, but I am encouraged about the possibility. I appreciate David's good thinking.

More about the planning process

Yesterday I introduced a diagram, shown again here, as a way of describing a dynamic planning process. I would like to take it further as I refine my thoughts about the dynamics between a broad vision and great detail.

Framework Thinking

I believe this is a useful guide in thinking about school systems and their relationship to their surrounding community. I will later apply the diagram to my discussion of planning for downtown Holland, hoping to identify a correlation with thinking about future school systems and their community context. It may be a bit of a stretch, but I'd like to try.

The diagram is meant to imply a cyclic process, the frequent iterations of which will scope out and reveal the greatest possible opportunities to solve a problem. (In my world the problem focus is

the shape of our physical environment.) Underlying the diagram is a continuum of a time scale: the past, the present, the near future, and the distant future. The diagram assumes some particular outcome precepts:

- The broader the perspective, the greater the chance for fresh ideas to emerge.

- The more ideas are interrelated, the greater the chance for their implementation.

- The earlier an idea is introduced into the process, the greater the leverage to influence change.

As we plan facilities for teaching and learning environments, the perspective should be as broad as possible. In this sense, I believe every school site ought to be a place about community. It is more than trees, lawns, and sports fields, although it includes these things. It is about opportunities to learn—a laboratory—for exploring local history, how drinking water is cleansed, why some plants flourish and others die, how paths help neighborhoods communicate, and on and on.

This perspective sharpened for me very dramatically one year when I was working with some handicapped kids and their parents to design their school grounds. The intent was to reveal to the kids what some of their larger world was like. The students were called "trainable" in terms of potentially becoming part of normal, everyday life. The school grounds were designed to symbolize or represent common experiences they would not normally have. For instance, the hill was a mountain. When they climbed the hill to a platform, they could see across to other parts of the community … or "the world." The paths were "streets" with traffic signs and crossing names. A "trip" ended with a wheelchair boardwalk from which the kids could fish in a small pond, which became their "waterfront." There were a whole series of experiences of this kind and both the kids and their parents loved it. In fact, the parents were motivated to build many of the features.

With this experience, I came to realize that this rather forlorn school site, designed with ideas emanating from the kids, their teachers, and their parents, was so much more significant than any school grounds I had yet experienced. It was all about listening to the kids and looking closer at our familiar places in order to see them more clearly and celebrate them more fully. It was not about more money for construction but more about ideas. In this case the site development costs turned out to be less than expected. I thought this point of view could be transferable to the planning of school sites so often devoted to only recreation.

Listening to the user

Another experience of this kind occurred in Chicago. It was a chance encounter with some people who were aware of a school grounds issue at DuSable High School on the south side of Chicago. They asked me to come to the school and talk to the kids who were thinking about how to make their school grounds safer and more useful. I did go and I met with a group of the high school students, some of their teachers, and the principal. The school grounds were like a blank sheet of paper—asphalt play areas and parking, desolate-looking and uninviting. But the kids considered it their place and they had images of something special. They were talking about finding some way of bringing some life to that school ground. Across the street were high-rise apartments. Nearby were older kids just waiting for the younger kids to get out of school. The students felt the school grounds were not safe … you know the story better than I do. We met in the cafeteria for lunch and a couple dozen students—tenth, eleventh, and twelfth graders—gathered to explain their ideas.

The students noted that the "authorized" program called for basketball courts and all the normal paraphernalia for a playground. It was going to be done right away. But the kids were saying that sports alone would not help … and they had some specific ideas about a better way.

I was asked to join them to help with the thinking and to illustrate the things they were talking about. So we gathered in the cafeteria around a couple of large illustration boards. They noted that if the school grounds were designed solely for kids' sports, the project would fail. But if the school grounds were designed to be attractive to their grandparents, the chances were good that kids could both play and be secure because, as one student explained, "Every time my grandma comes by the school, those guys on the street disappear."

Great thought! I picked up the chalks and asked them to say more about what they imagined might attract their grandparents. They talked. I made sketches on the site plan—little bird's-eye sketches and small site-plan vignettes. As they watched that blank paper become the place they were talking about, their fascination and interest grew.

Then an amazing thing happened. As I was drawing, a young girl came up and put her hand on my drawing hand and asked to see how such drawing feels. With her hand on mine, we drew together … she wanted to draw so badly. At first a bit hesitant, the rest of the kids finally crowded around this piece of paper. Each wanted to help shape this imaginary "grandparents park." Even some of the teachers pitched in. The principal seemed delighted. We got a couple more pads and had a fascinating two hours of drawing, thinking, and talking.

A conceptual scheme for the site took form that day. Others later refined the plan, and local contractors agreed to build it. The kids were the source for the ideas; they feel they helped shape it. My role as a professional was not as author, but as coach.

The Chicago experience reminded me that we often have preconceived notions about what ought to happen—a rigid kind of thinking. We need to learn to listen—not passively, but creatively. There is a way of listening that is an initiative, wherein the "things" people are thinking—the things they don't have the words for or cannot draw—are "encouraged" out of them. It takes skill, patience, and a forgiving attitude about process. The process at times needs to be more spontaneous, not so predetermined.

Spontaneity and creativity

Spontaneity is an important element in the iterative process I have outlined. Each of these pieces I have shown on my process diagram—vision, knowing the problem, knowing the place, knowing the people, producing ideas, and conceiving implementation strategies—is a formidable item for proper analysis. Each can involve volumes of material, potentially overwhelming in the magnitude of it all. But if one is clear enough about the fundamentals, one can very rapidly scurry through these pieces early in the game—out-of-order if need be—and discover the magic of their "interdependence."

"Thin slices" produce creative thinking! That's how ideas are found, and ideas are power.

I want to stress that the worth of this process, as creative and productive as it is, can only be evaluated in terms of the outcome. The outcome and the process are inseparable. If the results are worthy, then so must be the process, and vice versa.

Many times the chosen process is so enticing and so dominant that it becomes an end in itself. Just to complete the process is a victory. But the process is only the vehicle. If the process can be simple, then let it be simple. If it reaches a worthy conclusion early, then take that conclusion and move on. The process doesn't always have to be completed in its totality if it begins to produce the things you want it to produce.

The Downtown Holland story

This attitude about the planning process was my perspective when, in 1988, I was invited by Dr. Gordon Van Wylen to come to Holland to work with a private-sector planning group that was seeking to promote and guide the renewal of Holland's downtown. It turned out to be a great opportunity to apply this philosophy, and I would like to use the Holland story to illustrate it. Please know these remarks come from my particular bias and from only a limited view of a much larger picture.

Two key people greeted me on my arrival, Gordon and his

colleague Greg Holcombe. Gordon Van Wylen, a respected philosopher about people and place, who served as president of Hope College, is a person in whom this community has enormous trust. His role was to communicate to others the vision of Downtown Holland as a destination center. Greg Holcombe is a young, extremely capable community planner who had the role of keeping the process well managed and moving forward. My role was to help shape and illustrate the ideas aimed at making the vision a reality. Drawing pictures to show people what they were thinking and therein discovering fresh ideas was familiar to me and I relished the opportunity.

Early in my involvement I met Edgar Prince, who frequently conferred with the planning team. It was clear he was the motivating force for the initiative. Ed Prince was a most remarkable person, a successful industrialist who cared enormously about this community. One of his comments when I first met him was, "This is a town you can get hold of and keep it special." He added that larger cities can be overwhelming in magnitude and complexity. In effect, Ed Prince was saying that when one can "get hold of a place," a place with history, roots, and coherence, then one wants to do everything one can to protect it. He was very excited about this notion because, as an innovator, he wanted to make things happen. He was action oriented. He was ill at ease with the slowness of government procedures. He felt the public planning process was often so long-term that a vision was easily lost in the process. So the private initiative team of Gordon, Greg, and Ed successfully combined a deliberate and thorough overview process with action-oriented innovation. Over the next few years this private initiative in downtown planning became an effective partner with the public initiative—a special kind of private-public partnership.

Three terms were central to the early efforts in my involvement: inform, involve, inspire. Without making much of it as a formal process, we followed these three reminders very carefully.

Number one: "inform." Gather the pertinent information and present it in ways that make key aspects of it quickly understandable. It's all about knowing the place.

Second: "involve, involve, involve." You can get things done if the stakeholders are motivated to do it.

The third is crucial: "inspire." Make sure ideas about change result. Shape them in ways that are lucid, interesting, and achievable. When people get excited about their place, enthused about being involved, and inspired about change-making ideas, just about anything can be accomplished.

That's why I mentioned the little subdivision in my first talk. Those people knew their place well and became deeply involved in the process, and had clear ideas on how to save their place. And they did the seemingly impossible. Likewise, the people of Holland came up against the grain of everything that's happening in our country and brought back Holland's downtown to the vitality you see. It was grassroots stuff. Ed Prince and Gordon Van Wylen, along with other merchants and investors, professionals like myself, and citizen groups, were well informed and involved. And ideas about change were always given prime attention.

A number of citizens, including Ed Prince, joined together to form a private investment group to provide capital for the acquisition of strategic land in the downtown area. The availability of this capital gave important leverage as the process unfolded. This initial step was essentially a private venture, quite independent of the city. Fairly soon, however, a close interaction with the city developed, and an effective partnership of private-public thinking evolved. This has been a great resource and strength over the past twelve years. The think-tanks about downtown issues are always joint efforts now, always interlaced with public-private synergy. It's a wonderful evolution of mutual confidence and trust, providing room for distinctive public and private developments.

I sense that you have already strolled the streets of downtown Holland. If so, you surely have come to appreciate the quality of the buildings (many of which go back to the turn of the century), the diversity and attractiveness of the shops, and the overall vitality of the downtown. What you may not perceive is the remarkable transformation that has taken place over the last twelve years. Prior to this period there was no major shopping mall in the area. Downtown

An alley—before
improvement.

A vision of
the alley's potential
for improvement.

Same alley—today—
showing how the
"backs" of buildings
have been turned into
pleasant shopping
walkways even as
they continue
to provide access
for service vehicles.

Holland was the retail shopping center of the community. There were the usual downtown banks, but most of the professionals—the doctors, dentists, and lawyers—had moved to new facilities outside the downtown area, leaving many of the second floors vacant. A mall was under construction a few miles away, and all the downtown department stores were moving to the mall. Holland faced the situation that has confronted countless American cities, where malls have drained the downtowns of their key features, leaving them essentially dead. Many have struggled valiantly to keep the downtown alive, but often it is a losing battle after so much of the downtown life has gone elsewhere. Fortunately, Holland's story is different. But this was the context in which I was invited to participate in a major effort to renew downtown Holland.

A brief overview of these efforts is illustrated with maps and some slides. This overview is not so much to tell the Holland story as it is to bring into focus some of the basic ideas I have been presenting to you, principles that I often use in addressing such issues. I hope you will gain both insight and inspiration that will be of help as you think creatively how you and your schools can be catalysts for renewed community vitality. As superintendents and principals, you are in unique positions to play leadership roles in such endeavors, as many of you already do.

I hope that you will sense how this process unfolded. It was rather low-key—no dramatic "master plan" talk. For many it may have seemed to be a series of seemingly unrelated pieces of building. But it was a careful strategy based on a clearly stated vision, giving each piece its reason for being.

And the process is still unfolding. It is not going to stop, for the process functions like a reciprocal engine, with the vision inspiring the details, and the details informing the vision.

Two things were important as a starting point. One was that this was an essentially sound community, having been founded more than 150 years ago in accordance with a great community plan. This relates to my earlier comment that our forefathers were able to plan great towns. When I hear individuals in our market economy say one ought to be free to do anything one wants with their property, I am dismayed. The implication is that a plan limits individual property rights. But most town plans of the eighteenth and nineteenth centuries in this country were thoughtful, deliberate, and orderly. Such plans were not limits … they were inspirations. Today we admire their enduring qualities. To the pioneers it was good business to make careful plans.

Holland has the heritage of a great town plan. Centennial Park is a beautiful example: a tree-filled central green bounded on one side by City Hall and Herrick Library, on another side by the downtown business district, on another by Hope College, and on the last by what is now an historic residential neighborhood. This has been a wonderful center of events for the annual Tulip Festival and many other community events, a site carefully thought through 150 years ago. The roads are in a typical Midwest grid pattern, leading one directly to the water, to the Farmers Market, or to the railroad station A simple grid has the advantage of providing many alternate routes to any destination in the city.

The second thing already on the table when I arrived twelve years ago was a vision for downtown, represented in the minds of a few key leaders who had the trust of the community. In this vision they conceived of a certain kind of wholeness. It can be summed up like this: Downtown Holland was already an attractive shopping place. But the vision was that it could be better by re-thinking it in terms of the downtown being a destination center rather than simply a retail center. A destination center implies that we need to have more mixed uses here than normal. The historical tradition was that "downtown" was primarily the place to shop and to do government business. But the new vision conceived of a residential-life ingredient that would shift the character of downtown from "stop and shop" to "stay and enjoy." It becomes a quality-of-life target. If one achieved a high quality-of-living downtown, one also would increase shopping quality, security, workplace quality, and the simple overall enjoyment of delightful events in an intriguing place.

As the vision was first described to me, the thinking was not about downtown as two retail blocks. The thinking was about a whole place, including the Hope College campus, the neighborhoods, the public places, and the businesses. Because of that broad vision, all dimensions of downtown have been and will continue to be touched, improved, and expanded as needed.

So two things were in place—a great town and a clear vision. The private sector group was willing and ready to do things if they knew what to do. At that time a local effort of the National Main Street program, which had been in place for four years, was having its impact. A major effort, called Streetscape, was under way to replace the streets, sidewalks, lighting, and amenities in downtown. Ed Prince contributed a brilliant idea. Holland has considerable snow in the winter. So while the streets were all torn up, he suggested putting some of the waste heat from the nearby municipal power plant under the streets and sidewalks of the downtown so when winter came, ice and snow would never form.

This feature would remove a major deterrent to effective shopping throughout the winter. It wasn't easy. Ed and those working with him were aware of a creative Swedish snow-melt system. The city, of course, as is often the case with the public sector, indicated it was not possible and explained why it couldn't be done. But Ed Prince was undeterred. He was the type of person who asks, "Why not?" If asked "when?" Ed would look at his watch rather than his calendar. It was that kind of energy that led to the installation of a snow-melt system extending three blocks, store front to store front. A unique investment was made almost overnight because a private sector partner worked with the city government. Since the Streetscape project has been finished, people invariably say, "Wow! Isn't this place great!"

And ideas for other downtown functions emerged, such as quality office buildings, restaurants, and residential spaces, bringing additional life to the town. Each in turn would attract more business activity and spawn the next idea. What began to take shape was a more vital and more attractive downtown. Increased residential life was an important part of the energy. Ed Prince and his wife, Eisa, undertook a number of projects. Those projects were superbly done, financed from the Princes' own resources. The Princes were catalysts who inspired others to do the same.

At the same time, the Freedom Village initiative took form. The site was a small residential area of old, mostly run-down homes. The area was isolated from the rest of the community by the waterfront, railroad tracks, and older industrial buildings. The thought occurred that this would be an ideal site for a residential center for empty nesters and retirees. The homes were purchased with sensitivity regarding those who would be displaced. Also a largely abandoned factory was acquired. Today, Freedom Village is a very well-regarded life-care facility, with about 500 residents who can walk along the waterfront or stroll the downtown streets. A long waiting list of prospective residents testifies to the success of this major downtown residential development.

My involvement in the process has continued over the years. From the beginning I have emphasized quick and frequent turns of the planning cycle. No planning/design session was longer than two days; usually it was half a day. The team would go through the process quickly as I have described, address new issues, and produce new ideas to match. We would seek to know and understand the problem, get acquainted with who's involved, assess the obstacles, illustrate ideas to be considered, find reasonable ways to get it done, and check it out with the vision. When the answers spelled "go," it usually would be initiated the same day. During this time, the private sector purchased key parcels of real estate with the view of selling them in a way that would be consistent with the vision. The private sector's responsibility was enormous in terms of holding the land in reserve and working to put it into the right use at the right moment.

Some basic principles to consider

Framework Thinking. All of the foregoing leads me to note a most important guiding principle—what I call "framework think-ing"—that we carefully attended. It is akin to the service infrastruc-ture of the community, the familiar roadway, sewer, water, and power transmission systems. To this basic framework of services I like to add another kind of system I have been talking about: an inter-connect-ed open space, bikeway, and pedestrian system. Such an "open space system" point-of-view forms the physical framework *within* which we can place the many and varied functions and facilities serving our needs. The framework follows the vision and therefore, like the vision, becomes a constant, a pragmatic, physical reference point in the complex checkerboard of development. Without this framework, the assorted pieces of development would have no glue to hold things together.

Make Connections. This key principle permeated our thinking as the process evolved. It responds to the issue that our world is increasingly disconnected. There are few places of significance to which we can walk from our homes with safety. We drive everywhere, often in heavy traffic where aggressive drivers try our commitment to noble actions. We are trapped in centers of beauty, such as our home, and then are trapped in our cars as we drive to the mall only to be trapped in the mall itself, and trapped again as we plunge into traffic en route to our next destination. There are few pleasant, enjoyable, safe connections between one destination and another. The overall result is discordance. Our disconnected environment must surely add to our impatience and lack of a sense of peace with others and ourselves.

Accordingly, we emphasized the creation of a safe and pleasant interconnected system of pedestrian movement. The walking environment along Eighth Street through the retail and office district was already newly built and a big hit. Certain other streets, like College and Columbia, were chosen to have walkways that were given special attention. They connect Hope College through the vibrant retail shopping area to the new waterfront along the Macatawa River delta, including Freedom Village. Another connecting system was between the Hope campus and the City Hall and the Library via beautiful Centennial Park. This attractive connecting system, enabling people to easily walk from one destination to another, has proven to be a key element in downtown Holland's success.

The connection idea has grown. Downtown Holland's emphasis on connections spread to the larger community through the concept of trails for walkers and bikers along the wooded Macatawa

These overview sketches are typical of the *charrette*
process used in planning Holland's downtown.

River Greenway System. The greenway trail is intended to connect
the northeast neighborhoods through the northern boundary of
downtown all the way to Lake Macatawa on the west. These walk-
ways/trails will strengthen the identity and sense of connection for
several surrounding downtown neighborhoods. In turn downtown
will be strengthened by such direct relationships. Greg Holcombe is
playing a leadership role in planning the extended system, and significant progress is being made to implement these ideas.

Clusters in the Mix. Another important principle in our thinking was the general clustering of functions, yet with careful mixed-use features. City Hall, the adjacent public library, and Centennial Park comprise an essential cluster of public functions within an events/recreation theme. The shops and art galleries are clustered on the main street, and office buildings are clustered on cross streets behind or above retail stores. The Hope College campus, with its clusters of residence halls, academic buildings, and athletic facilities, has the character of the compact, mixed-use environment we were seeking for downtown.

Integrating the principles of "framework," "connections," and "clusters" can do much to strengthen the coherence of a complex community.

The *"Charrette."* A very effective way to efficiently move things along in the planning process is an event called a *"charrette."* Borrowed from the French Beaux Artes design tradition, a charrette has become architectural jargon for an intense, short-term workshop, usually two or three days, that is used to gain insight and ideas from many participants. Usually a charrette will focus on a given place or

Sculpture, such as this one given by Ed and Elsa Prince, adds to the pleasant intimacy so many enjoy about downtown Holland.

Restored historic buildings add to the charm of Holland's
downtown.

issue within the conceptual framework. The leaders of a charrette are
professionals—architects, planners, builders—but the overall purpose is gaining the insights, ideas, and concerns of many interests.

We have organized several informal charrettes for downtown
Holland and the city has also sponsored several workshops of a more
formal kind. People from all sorts of backgrounds come to express

their ideas. It's a chance to pitch in with questions such as "Why can't you do such-and-such?" or "We don't understand the concept," or a comment like "We really support this idea." I have never been nervous about my role as a designer being circumvented by a citizen designer. Design is not magic. All design is about creating a new phenomenon based on information about place and people. The response simply forms ideas—and that's design. A charrette provides the concentrated time and organization to pack the thinking tightly together. The immediate product is usually an illustrated record of insights—a booklet of ideas quickly produced with a copy machine for distribution. The results are not meant to be final but rather to stir the imagination toward more definitive plans. If people help to design their own place, they become advocates, and it will be much more likely to happen.

One of the most important dimensions of the creative planning that took place in downtown Holland was a public/private partnership marked by a common vision, open communication, mutual trust, and an openness to new ideas. One of our important mottoes was, "There is no limit to what we can do together if we don't care who gets the credit." The beauty of what has and is happening in Holland is that the plan did not come down from on high. The basic guiding force was the vision and the conceptual framework. But the details of the plan are continually unfolding through daily attention to current issues, emergent needs, and new players. It is not prescribing a "master" plan that people need to vote on. As intended, the Downtown Holland story keeps forming each day toward the ends so well described in the vision.

As I have noted earlier, I believe there is an important synergy between our school systems and the overall quality of life of a community. The more we think about the two as an interrelated set of phenomena, the better. I believe the best of that synergy can be captured by a creative, inclusive planning approach similar in spirit and content to that which I have tried to illustrate.

As you think about the future of your school systems, I hope and trust that the important relationships with the community can be better identified and lead to the forging of stronger connections. It could be of great benefit to your students, your teachers, your resources, and your entire community.

Notes

Chapter 3

1. Sophocles, "Antigone" (442 B.C.), trans. Emil Braun (New York: Oxford University Press, 1990), 1.277.

2. See Robert N. Bellah, *The Broken Covenant: American Civil Religion in a Time of Trial* (Boston: Seabury, 1975).

3. U.S. Bureau of the Census, *American Almanac*, Table No. 87, p. 73; Andrew J. Cherlin, *Marriage, Divorce, Remarriage,* (Cambridge, Mass.: Harvard University Press, 1992, rev. ed.), 22. Over a longer period, the shift in marital patterns is also dramatic. Of marriages that occurred during the 1920s, for example, approximately 20 percent have resulted (or are expected to result) in divorce. Of marriages initiated in the 1950s, this proportion is approximately 30 percent. And of marriages initiated in the 1970s or 1980s, it exceeds 50 percent. In keeping with the extent to which they value family, most divorced people remarry, and many of those who divorce a second time also remarry. The important trend, however, is that the symbolic and legal boundary separating marriage and nonmarriage is being crossed more often; put simply, marriage is no longer a bond that is inviolable. Explanations for the rising divorce rate that find greatest empirical support include ones that emphasize economic conditions that require women to participate in the paid labor force, movement of jobs that undermine the economic status of certain segments of the male population, and geographic mobility or other shifts away from traditional family and community

support systems; see Sara McLanahan and Lynne Casper, "Growing Diversity and Inequality in the American Family," *State of the Union: America in the 1990s,* vol. 2, *Social Trends,* ed. Reynolds Farley (New York: Russell Sage Foundation, 1995), 1–46. These explanations suggest the relatedness of various manifestations of what I am calling porous institutions. McLanahan and Casper also cite evidence on family patterns in other advanced industrialized societies that shows these changes are not limited to the United States.

4. USA Today/CNN/Gallup Poll conducted in February 1997.

5. Source: General Social Surveys, 1973–96; Harris Survey, 1971, question: "I'm going to name some institutions in this country. As far as the people running these institutions are concerned, would you say you have a great deal of confidence, only some confidence, or hardly any confidence at all in them?"

6. Francis Fukuyama, *Trust: The Social Virtues and the Creation of Prosperity* (New York: Free Press, 1995).

7. Robert Wuthnow, *God and Mammon in America* (New York: Free Press, 1994), 173.

8. Gallup Poll (August 12, 1996).

9. Time/CNN/Yankelovich Survey (January 1997).

10. Survey of American Political Culture, conducted by the Gallup Organization in 1996 for James Davison Hunter at the University of Virginia.

11. U.S. Bureau of the Census, *Statistical Abstract of the United States: 1996* (Washington, D.C.: Government Printing Office, 1996), Table Nos. 337–40.

12. For the full time series, see Putnam, "Bowling Alone," Figure 11.

13. See especially Wade Clark Roof, *Generation of Seekers* (San Francisco: Harper, 1993).

14. Survey of American Political Culture.

15. Ibid.

16. Wuthnow, *God and Mammon in America*.

17. Robert Wuthnow, *Learning to Care* (New York: Oxford University Press, 1995).

18. Frank Dobbin, *Forging Industrial Policy* (Cambridge: Cambridge University Press, 1994).

References

Chapters 1 and 2

Elliott, David J. *Music Matters: A New Philosophy of Music Education.* New York: Oxford University Press, 1995.

Chapter 5

Caro, Robert A. *The Power Broker: Robert Moses and the Fall of New York.* New York: Random House, 1975.

Ellfers, Joost, and Robert Green. *The 48 Laws of Power.* New York: Viking Press, 1998.

Jones, Laurie B. *Jesus CEO: Using Ancient Wisdom for Visionary Leadership.* New York: Hyperion Books, 1996.

Yates, Martin. *Hiring the Best.* Holbrook, Mass.: Adams Media, 1993.

Chapter 8

Harris, Judith Rich. *The Nurture Assumption.* New York: Free Press, 1998.

Myers, David G. The American Paradox. New Haven, Conn.: Yale University Press, 2000.

Chapter 9

Gardner, John. *Excellence: Can We Be Equal and Excellent Too?* New York: W. W. Norton, 1995.

Kunstler, James. *Home from Nowhere: Remaking Our Everyday World for the Twenty-First Century.* New York: Simon & Schuster, 1996.

1999
Van Andel Educators Institute

Lecturers

Beverly L. Hall
State District Superintendent
Superintendent (July 1, 1999)

Newark Public Schools
Newark, New Jersey
Atlanta Public Schools
Atlanta, Georgia

G. Christian Jernstedt
Professor, Department of
Psychological and Brain Sciences

Dartmouth College
Hanover, New Hampshire

William Johnson
Professor Emeritus of
    Landscape Architecture
Former Dean, School of Natural Resources

University of Michigan
Ann Arbor, Michigan

David G. Myers
John Dirk Werkman
    Professor of Psychology

Hope College
Holland, Michigan

Ronald J. Sjoerdsma
Professor of Education
Director, Van Andel Educational
    Technology School
Van Andel Education Institute

Calvin College
Grand Rapids, Michigan

Maribeth Vander Weele   Chicago Public Schools
Inspector General   Chicago, Illinois

Nicholas Wolterstorff   Yale University
Noah Porter Professor of   Cambridge, Connecticut
  Philosophical Theology
Fellow, Berkeley College

Robert Wuthnow   Princeton University
Gerhard R. Andlinger   Princeton, New Jersey
  Professor of Social Sciences
Director, Center for the Study of Religion

Moderators

Nancy Miller   Hope College
Dean for the Social Sciences   Holland, Michigan

P. Douglas Kindschi   Grand Valley State University
Dean of Science and Mathematics   Allendale, Michigan

Beverly Hall   Atlanta Public Schools
Superintendent of Schools   Atlanta, Georgia

Participants

Michael J. Bina   Indiana School of the Blind
Superintendent   Indianapolis, Indiana

Lawrence M. Bowman   Diocese of Covington
Superintendent of Schools   Covington, Kentucky

Tracy L. Cross   Ball State University
Executive Director   Muncie, Indiana
Indiana Academy for Science
Mathematics & Humanities

Jan Dalman   Holland Public Schools
Assistant Superintendent for Instruction   Holland, Michigan

James Den Ouden   Bellflower Christian Schools
Superintendent   Bellflower, California

Mary E. Devin   Geary County Schools
Superintendent   Junction City, Kansas

John Emery   Phillipsburg School District
Superintendent   Phillipsburg, Pennsylvania

Rosemary Ervine   West Ottawa Public Schools
Superintendent   Holland, Michigan

Thomas R. Giblin   East Lansing Public Schools
Superintendent   East Lansing, Michigan

Colleen G. Goltz   Ada Public Schools
                                                   Ada, Minnesota

Richard Hanks   National School District
Principal   National City, California

James F. Hatch   Zeeland High School
Principal   Zeeland, Michigan

Edgar B. Hatrick   Loudon County Public Schools
Superintendent   Leesburg, Virginia

LeRoy E. Hay
Assistant Superintendent
for Instruction

Wallingford Public Schools
Wallingford, Connecticut

Caroline Jones
Director

Prairie Creek Community School
Northfield, Minnesota

David J. Koetje
Superintendent

Grand Rapids Christian Schools
Grand Rapids, Michigan

Debbie McFalone
Assistant Superintendent

Grand Rapids Public Schools
Grand Rapids, Michigan

Raymond J. McNulty
Superintendent

Windham Southeast Supervisory Union
Brattleboro, Vermont

James O'Donnell
Superintendent

Diocese of Grand Rapids Catholic Schools
Grand Rapids, Michigan

Kevin O'Neill
Superintendent

Coopersville Area Public Schools
Coopersville, Michigan

Charles Pasma
Superintendent

Bellevue Christian School
Clyde Hill, Washington

Jack Postma
Principal

Unity Christian School
Hudsonville, Michigan

Mary Ann Reynolds
Associate Superintendent
for Administration

Fort Bend Intermediate School District
Houston, Texas

Roberto L. Santos
Assistant Superintendent

United Independent School District
Laredo, Texas

James W. Scott
Superintendent

Spring Cove Area School District
Roaring Spring, Pennsylvania

Gary M. Smit   Lombard School District 44
Superintendent   Lombard, Illinois

Edward Torres   Kensington High School
Principal   Philadelphia, Pennsylvania

Dennis Van Andel   Rehoboth Christian School
Superintendent   Rehoboth, New Mexico

Michael S. Weiler   Sparta Area Schools
Superintendent   Sparta, Michigan